Maurice Prendergast 1859-1924

Verso: Photograph of Maurice Prendergast about 1914. Courtesy the Whitney Museum of American Art

MUSEUM OF FINE ARTS : BOSTON

Maurice

PRENDERGAST

1859-1924

BY

HEDLEY HOWELL RHYS

HARVARD UNIVERSITY PRESS : CAMBRIDGE

(1960)

EXHIBITION SCHEDULE

MUSEUM OF FINE ARTS, BOSTON	October 26 – December 4, 1960
WADSWORTH ATHENEUM, HARTFORD	December 29, 1960 – February 5, 1961
WHITNEY MUSEUM OF AMERICAN ART, NEW YORK	February 21 – April 2, 1961
CALIFORNIA PALACE OF THE LEGION OF HONOR, SAN FRANCISCO	April 22 – June 3, 1961
CLEVELAND MUSEUM OF ART	June 20 – July 30, 1961

All Rights Reserved.   Library of Congress Catalogue Card No. 60-16756

Printed in West Germany by Brüder Hartmann, Berlin.   Designed by Carl F. Zahn, Boston Museum.

Published by Museum of Fine Arts, Boston and Harvard University Press, Cambridge, October 1960.

Acknowledgment

The preparation of this book and the memorial exhibition on which it is based has demanded the generous assistance of a few devoted friends of the Museum of Fine Arts and sacrifice on the part of many lenders, both museums and private collectors. Our special thanks are due to Mrs. Charles Prendergast, Mr. Robert Brady and Miss Antoinette Kraushaar for helpful advice and for their graciousness in placing invaluable records at our disposal. To the collectors and museums listed below we owe a debt of thanks for their loans and for their generous permission to reproduce the paintings and prints included in this volume.   P. T. R.

Mr. and Mrs. William T. Aldrich
Mr. and Mrs. Arthur G. Altschul
Mrs. William Hayes Bender, Jr.
Robert Brady
Mr. and Mrs. Henry W. Breyer, Jr.
Walter P. Chrysler, Jr.
Mr. and Mrs. Donald G. Crowell
Mr. and Mrs. Charles C. Cunningham
Mrs. Alfred Curtis
Miss Daphne Dunbar
Mr. and Mrs. Walter Fillin
Mr. and Mrs. William Marshall Fuller
Mr. and Mrs. Nelson Goodman
Mr. and Mrs. John G. Greene
Mr. and Mrs. George Greenspan
Dr. and Mrs. MacKinley Helm

Joseph H. Hirshhorn
Dr. and Mrs. Ernest Kahn
Mr. and Mrs. John Koch
Mrs. John F. Kraushaar
Mr. and Mrs. Henry Lee, Jr.
Dr. and Mrs. Irving Levitt
Dr. and Mrs. Paul Todd Makler
Mrs. Margarett Sargent McKean
Mrs. Sherman Miles
Mr. and Mrs. Roy R. Neuberger
Mr. and Mrs. Philip F. Newman
Mrs. Bliss Parkinson
Mrs. Edward Patterson
Mr. and Mrs. John G. Pierce
Mr. and Mrs. M. P. Potamkin
Miss Leona E. Prasse

(7)

LeMOYNE ART FOUNDATION, INC.
125 North Gadsden
Tallahassee, Florida 32301

Mrs. Charles Prendergast
Mr. and Mrs. Perry T. Rathbone
Mrs. Ethel Linder Reiner
Mrs. Stanely B. Resor
Mr. and Mrs. Walter L. Ress
Mr. and Mrs. Walter Ross
Mr. and Mrs. Harry Rubin
Mr. and Mrs. Ansley W. Sawyer, Jr.

Mr. and Mrs. Melvin Schifter
Winthrop Taylor
Mr. and Mrs. Alan H. Temple
Mr. and Mrs. Richard K. Weil
Oliver Williams
Mrs. Oliver E. Williams
Mr. and Mrs. Ralph L. Wilson

Addison Gallery of American Art, *Andover*
Albright Art Gallery, *Buffalo*
Art Institute of Chicago
Museum of Fine Arts, *Boston*
Butler Institute of American Art, *Youngstown, Ohio*
Cleveland Museum of Art
Des Moines Art Center
Detroit Institute of Arts
Lehigh University, *Bethlehem, Pennsylvania*
Metropolitan Museum of Art, *New York*
Minneapolis Institute of Arts
Mt. Holyoke College, *South Hadley, Massachusetts*
Museum of Modern Art, *New York*
Nelson Gallery – Atkins Museum, *Kansas City, Missouri*
Phillips Collection, *Washington, D. C.*
Santa Barbara Museum of Art
City Art Museum of St. Louis
Smith College Museum of Art, *Northampton, Massachusetts*
Society for the Preservation of New England Antiquities, *Boston*
Museum of Fine Arts, *Springfield, Massachusetts*
Toledo Museum of Art
Whitney Museum of American Art, *New York*
(8)   Worcester Art Museum

Contents

60   REVERE BEACH   about 1896

Foreword

"The love you liberate in your work is the only love you keep." Obedient to the habit of years, Maurice Prendergast jotted down this philosophic reflection in a sketchbook in 1905. Every painting and every print he ever did proclaim that he lived by this idealistic and pure precept. In a freshet of instinctive color and disciplined form he liberated a simple, untroubled love for the world he chose to see. His vision will endure, but during his lifetime it won him only a small circle of admirers. Recently this recognition has widened so steadily and so far that Prendergast, who came to expect little of buyers, would have found it hard to credit the number who now find joy and deep satisfaction in seeing through his eyes, in sharing the love he "kept."

A century has passed since the birth of Maurice Prendergast in 1859. This book and the exhibition on which it is based have been prepared to honor that anniversary, to record his achievement and his unique contribution to American art.

Yet this celebration is significant in respect not only to time but to place as well. Boston was the home of Maurice Prendergast for all but twelve years of his life. That the Boston Museum should have the honor of initiating this observance would seem self-evident. But the honor it assumes has deeper import: the Museum frankly seeks the grace of a redeeming act. If Prendergast found discouragingly little patronage on the part of museums elsewhere, it was painfully the case at home. In a great museum where the work of other Boston artists abounds, the paintings of Maurice Prendergast found no representation during his lifetime and have until recently been in very short supply. This memorial will help to repay a debt long owed to him.

In historic retrospect the experience of Prendergast in Boston as an artist with but little honor in his home town was rare. For Boston has in one way or another done rather well by her painter sons both native and adopted. Earlier painters such as Copley, Allston, Stuart, Harding, Hunt and Homer found abundant favor and patronage. As for Prendergast's two contemporaries, Sargent was idolized; while there was an insatiable demand for the brisk, impressionistic water colors of Dodge Macknight. (11)

Yet Prendergast had to apply himself to frame carving and to designing show cards in order to eke out a living. Why should Prendergast's paintings have attracted in his lifetime the attention of only three or four patrons when today collectors would have awaited with impatience each new group of water colors, every latest canvas from his easel? In one sense, the answer is simple. The experience of Prendergast was the typical experience of the non-academic artist in the early twentieth century. His fashionable contemporaries, and the artists who preceded him, practised an art that was basically realistic, whether it was dictated by the portrait requirements of a provincial English society as brilliantly reflected in the art of Copley and Stuart, whether it was the romantic realism of Allston evoking a world of imagination, or the poetic realism of William Morris Hunt with its humanist emphasis derived from Millet, or yet the virtuoso objectivity of Sargent.

Prendergast alone in his milieu stood for the new direction art was to take in the twentieth century. Indeed, in this respect he was distinguished from all his contemporaries, even from his painter comrades – the insurgent Eight – whom he later joined in New York. Unlike every one of them he thought of nature primarily as a point of departure. Instead of a realistic interpretation of the world, he adopted a schematic one. The reality he sought was not a transcript of natural appearances, not the Impressionists' transitory effect of light and atmosphere, but a more enduring reality arising from the "remembered image," an image refined by simplification, rhythmic organization, translation into a personal idiom of dots and patches of brushwork, an image sublimated by his own exquisite sense of color.

Prendergast's world is largely a peaceful world of holiday; a parade of picnics and beach parties, of summer outings, excursion crowds, of Sunday afternoons in the park. It is paradoxical that this beguiling spectacle with its sunlit charm, its light-hearted gaiety – the creation of a shy and modest man – should have been the spearhead in America of a radical artistic development. At the very time that Sargent, with customary brilliance, was pushing the plein-air water color to a quintescence of verisimilitude by touring Italy and Switzerland with folding easel, paint box and umbrella, Prendergast was quietly and faithfully pioneering a new direction in art. Locked in his studio, his color sketchbooks at hand filled with spontaneous, enchanting notations from nature, Prendergast was refining and organizing what he remembered and building his compositions according to the dictates of his imagination.

(12)

In the historical development of modern art this lonely citizen of Boston has a significance which has yet to be recognized. He was the harbinger for America of the revolutionary course of painting in the twentieth century.

Prendergast had gone to Paris at just the moment when Gauguin's revolt against the objectivity of Impressionism was creating a stir in artistic circles. The Frenchman's tenet that form resides not in nature but in the imagination and that color exists to be used in its prismatic purity and for its decorative value had caught the allegiance of the youthful group of Symbolists, the Nabis, notably Bonnard, Vuillard and Denis. From them Prendergast eagerly imbibed his first inspiration. Although other factors contributed to the gradual formation of his personal style, it was the example of this untried, rebellious fountainhead of modern painting that liberated his sensibilities and that set him on the course he was to follow unswervingly. In consequence, Prendergast was the first American who deliberately cast aside a strictly representational approach to art, used pure color as a formal element, permitted artistic means to dominate the subject matter. In a word, he was the first of his countrymen to admit the primacy of imagination and to abide by the basic principles which were to govern the vital art of the twentieth century.

PERRY T. RATHBONE
Director

Museum of Fine Arts
Boston
October, 1960

(14)　　　　　　　　38　EIGHT BATHERS　1916–18

Maurice B. Prendergast

1859-1924

by

HEDLEY HOWELL RHYS

MAURICE BRAZIL PRENDERGAST was America's first modern painter; a twentieth century artist born in the middle decade of the last century. The result of such prematurity was, inevitably, a long delayed recognition. His significance for American art could not be appreciated until the nineteenth century taste for realism had begun to decline. Now, at long last, in the middle of the twentieth century, his importance is fully recognized. He was in advance of his time in his concept of painting which for him was a sensuous means of expressing emotion, not only a way of recording appearances. His unique achievement in painting is the product of a constant search for adequate means. When he first was able to give all his energies to art, the most suitable means at hand were the techniques of the French Impressionists and their immediate followers. However, he differed from them in that he did not think of color as a formula for painting light, nor of painting as a dissected analysis of visual sensation. He discovered the poetic possibilities of Impressionism, and eventually used it as a lyrical instrument for a very personal poetry. This subjectivity is another aspect of his modernity. His artistic strength was his ability to transform all techniques and methods, wherever found, into an unique style entirely his own. This transformation created an art that is at once sensuous and spiritual.

Prendergast's singularity is most immediately felt in his fully developed style. Technically, the style demonstrates a solution to the problem of using broken tones and pure color simultaneously. Indeed, few have succeeded as well in uniting happily such a variety and encompassing range of color. Yet this harmony is not the product of a conscious theory, but is, rather, an expression of sensibility intended   (15) to recall a mood, to project a memory image, or to establish permanently a fleeting pleasure. Elusive joy is captured in an image of festive leisure, in scenes of never-ending holiday. Whether found on the beaches of New England, Normandy or Brittany, in New York's Central Park or on the boulevards of Paris, along the canals of Venice or on the piazzas of Rome and Siena, the subject of his painting is always a secure and innocent joy. This simple, ever recurring theme assumes an endless pictorial variety. A large collection of his work reveals the artistic transformations of the theme, the originality of the innovations, and the consistency of his development toward a personal and expressive art. His late monumental oils – so brilliantly represented at the Barnes Foundation in Merion, Pennsylvania – are not only summations of past experiences, but also explorations of a new realm of feeling. Though still festive, the processions that move across these canvases have a new significance. The bright, light colors have the quietude of complete concord; the figures have become almost formal and have about them an air of ritualistic pantomime. The innocent joy has been touched with nostalgia; naïveté and sophistication are fused.

A sense of childlike ingenuousness, a mood of simple gaiety, occasionally tinged with wistfulness, all conveyed by a complete control of the intricate color combinations and linear patterns, are the most consistent characteristics of Prendergast's art. From his work he would appear to have been part inspired child and part sophisticated aesthete, a duality implied in other records too. Among his friends, fellow artists and patrons his personality became something of a legend even within his own lifetime. Sometimes the legend was appreciated where his work was not. Those who knew him slightly stressed a childlike simplicity and its attributes. In their recollections of him they always referred to his naïveté and adolescent idealism, to his unrealistic attitude toward money and his inability to recognize harsh realities even when confronted with them in the forms of poverty and ill health; and always they remembered his gentle humor. His consuming passion for painting was offered as a partial explanation for this extraordinary insulation. Those who knew him well agreed with the others about his humor and his dedication to art, but they were also aware of his maturity and his complexity. To them his naïveté was a conscious conservation of simplicity, his attitude toward money the result of a mature value judement, and his insulation against harsh realities the product of a refusal to let them interfere with his fixed aims. As his brother Charles said of him: "Monny [Maurice] had the right idea. He knew he wanted to be an artist right from the start, and he didn't let anything stand in his way."

His numerous sketchbooks confirm the deeper dimension his more intimate friends perceived. The books were used for many things besides sketching. Everything went into them haphazardly: color notes and addresses, philosophical speculations and admonitions to drink less coffee, monetary records and a bibliography entitled "Dionysian Writers," thrice rewritten drafts of letters, and everywhere quotation after quotation from what he had been reading. He must have read voraciously. From his later sketchbooks it is evident that he read French easily and was not afraid of attacking German. His friend, Miss Daphne Dunbar of Boston, has remarked that in spite of his deafness he could get along quite well conversationally in French and that he knew the works of the great Russian authors. His comment after reading Tolstoi's religious writings was: "God would have made a good painter." However, the writers most frequently quoted are Nietzsche and the English romantic poets, Shelley, Coleridge and Byron, all in that order. Nietzsche's *The Birth of Tragedy*, from which the list of "Dionysian Writers" was probably culled, and his essay "Joyful Wisdom" seem to have been read many times. Passages from them are transcribed repeatedly between the years 1906 and 1912. Oddly enough, this rich fare did not taint his taste for the transparently simple. Jotted down cheek by jowl with Germanic profundities are such jingles as Kipling's "If a man would be successful in his art, art, art, He must keep the girls away from his heart, heart, heart." And from some unknown source comes: "Tell me pretty maid, whither are you going? The bark spreads its sails and the breeze is blowing." These two seem to have been great favorites. They both appear more than once. Here, sharply juxtaposed in these spasmodic journals are the simplicity and sophistication which his painting unites with such singular effect.

The plentiful but jumbled fragments in his sketchbooks reveal something of the quality of his mind and character. When pieced together, they are a moving record of Maurice's struggle for self betterment. Poverty he could ignore; deafness and uncertain health he could accept with his usual gentle humor. But what he felt most intensely was a need for a broader education than the austerity of his early youth had allowed. His search for knowledge was constant. Yet, on matters other than painting, (17)

141 FISHING PARTY 1900–05

he was never quite able to exorcise the lack of self-assurance which plagues the self-educated. This is poignantly felt in several drafts of a letter to Mrs. William Glackens. She had, obviously at a small dinner party, warned him about taking too seriously what he read in trashy newspapers. His first draft of the letter on the subject is self-deprecating, profuse in apology and touchingly grateful for her advice. Successive drafts become progressively more controlled and less self-revealing. The final one is a short, simple note thanking Mrs. Glackens for her interest and assuring her that he no longer read the offending newspaper. Jerome Meyers has described Maurice as he was at about the time of this letter. He saw him as a "short, white-haired, slight man, shut into his own world in a measure by his deafness." Charles Hovey Pepper, the Boston artist who somewhat earlier had painted the only known portrait of him, was won by his unpretentiousness: "Of all the men of genius I have known, Maurice Prendergast had the simplest manner. In conversation he showed the same naïve charm that is inherent in the lovely magic of his work." The uninhibited fragments in the sketchbooks suggest the wealth and variety of his private world and give a glimpse of the adult knowledge veiled by his ingenuous charm.

The motivating force behind Maurice's pursuit of learning was his dedication to art. All his reading, in no matter what field, was for the purpose of making him a better artist. Though the record of his reading is fragmentary, it is enough to indicate his wide knowledge of the history and traditions of his profession. He was in no sense a primitive; he was familiar with scholarly art journals, texts on Egyptian and ancient art, books on Giotto, Piero della Francesca, El Greco and many others. When this intensive study is added to his native gifts, his fresh vision and his sensitive response to color and line as active agents in themselves, it becomes apparent that he participated in modern art with a full consciousness of its significance. In the world of art his diffidence disappeared; there he was confident and at home. Max Weber says of a long talk he had with Maurice in 1912: "Conversation on art on this level or plane was rare and far between in those days." Ultimately, art was all of Maurice's life. He expressed his satisfaction with this condition in one of his innumerable quotations written in a sketchbook used as late as 1914: "Art is the great stimulus of life – I find it year by year more rich, more desirable, and more mysterious."

(19)

THE EARLY YEARS

Records of Maurice's childhood and early youth are very scarce. Until his brother's widow, Mrs. Charles Prendergast, discovered a family Bible, even the time and place of his birth were not clearly established. Statements by Maurice indicate that he tended to think of his life as beginning when he was brought to Boston in 1861. In the Bible it is recorded that he and his twin sister were born on October 10, 1859, according to his brother, in St. John's, Newfoundland. His father, Maurice Prendergast, was an Irishman who owned a trading post there. His mother, Mary Malvina Germaine, was of French Huguenot descent and came from Boston. When the business in St. John's failed in 1861, the whole family moved to Boston where the father earned a living for them by doing odd jobs. Charles, the second artist in the family, was born there on May 27, 1863. Both boys attended the Rice Grammar School on Dartmouth Street in Boston, and for both of them formal education was over at the age of fourteen. Maurice's first job was in a dry goods store where he seems to have spent most of his time sketching. The family did what they could to accomodate this artistic bent. They apprenticed him to a painter of show cards, where his chief duty was washing brushes, but by the time Charles left school in 1883 Maurice was supporting himself by lettering show cards. During these years the family lived in the South End of Boston and Maurice spent his free time in Day's Woods sketching landscapes with cattle. Years later Charles quipped: "In those days Maurice was hell on cows!" Sometime in 1884 these sketches came to the attention of Mrs. Waterbury, a minister's wife from Roxbury. She encouraged him, and advised him to go to Paris to study art when the time came. He was then twenty-five and the time still seemed very distant.

From his earliest boyhood Charles Prendergast seems to have been determined to help his brother become an artist. In the process he himself became a very distinguished one. His start was somewhat more auspicious. Upon leaving school he went to work for the art dealers Doll and Richards, then on Park Street, with whom he stayed for over two years. Then early one summer he left to work his passage to England and back on a cattle boat. The following summer, in 1886, he persuaded his older brother to accompany him on a similar voyage. This was Maurice's first European venture. Little remains of the work done on this trip; there is a drawing

(20)

in a sketchbook of a member of the ship's crew, and there is a water color of *Hawarden* in Wales, signed and dated 1886 (No. 49, ill. p. 140), that is a rather conventional rendering of an English thatched cottage amid trees. Addresses in the sketchbook are further evidence that the drawing was done somewhere near Chester on the Welsh border. The same sketchbook was used the following year in the environs of Boston for pen and ink drawings of landscapes. One bears the inscription: "May 1st, Everett, '87." In the summer of 1889 he spent a fortnight doing water colors at Brook's Cove, Westport Lower Landing, Maine. Three of these remain, one signed and dated (formerly in the collection of Mr. Arthur H. Jameson, Branford, Connecticut). After the first tentative European venture, life for Maurice became again the routine of his job lettering show cards, and the utilization of every spare moment away from it for his art. The major project in hand was to save enough money for a period of study in Paris. Toward this end Charles had become a salesman of brass and iron ware. They set themselves the goal of a thousand dollars, but they had been back from Europe five years before they achieved it.

The question of when Maurice first went to Paris is still a moot one. On the authority of a conversation with Charles, Mr. Van Wyck Brooks states specifically that Maurice arrived in Paris in May 1886, took a room in the Place Montparnasse, and later moved to an artist's lodging house in the Rue Campagne Première. He could quite readily have gone on to France from England that year. If he did, his first contact with Paris had no observable effect upon his work, probably because the contact was too brief. No work that he did there has yet come to light, and he was certainly sketching in Everett, Massachusetts, in May 1887. Neither these sketches nor the water colors he painted in Maine in 1889 show any important technical or stylistic difference from the water color done in Wales in 1886. All this work has a somewhat timid, self-taught character; the drawing is restrained, the color muted, and only once is the human figure attempted. Composition and technique seem to have been suggested by the book and magazine illustrations of the period. Only a nascent lyricism and an interest in sailing craft suggest the direction of his future development. The scarcity of work from this period in his life makes any conclusion hazardous. However, the scarcity may be due not only to the attrition of the years, but also to the fact he was then actually only a spare time artist. His effective career as a painter had not yet begun. This required for its impetus a much more (21) extended contact with the School of Paris than he had been able to achieve up to this point.

FRANCE

Maurice Prendergast was twenty-five when it was first suggested to him that he should study in Paris. He was past thirty before the suggestion became a reality. With indispensable help from Charles he was finally able to leave for France, where he was already at work by January 1891 (No. 50, ill. p. 140), and to stay there for over three years. In Paris he first studied under Courtois at Colarossi's, but soon moved to the life class at the Académie Julian where he worked under Constant, Blanc and Jean Paul Laurens. There he disregarded the advice of Laurens that he should study from the antique, and worked only from life. In the afternoons he worked at the cafés sketching the life in movement of the boulevards and the parks, a theme that, with variations in setting, was to persist throughout his career. In the work up to 1889 there had been an almost total absence of human figures; now there is an absorbed concentration upon the endless variety of their gestures and movements.

His first published works were sketches of this type, but unfortunately he received no credit for them. A young Englishman visited his studio and walked off with a book of them, took them to London and brought them to the attention of Whistler who recognized their quality and used his influence to have them published in *The Studio*. There they appeared in the 1893 volume to illustrate an article called "The Sketch Book in the Street," and are credited to one Michael Dignam. They represent women standing and in motion. The extreme freedom of the line, the swift rendering of the swirl of the voluminous skirts, and the combination of wit and elegance that has been elicited from the fantastic silhouettes of the costumes of the period are all unmistakably Maurice Prendergast. With his usual good humor, he refused to make a fuss about the theft.

The progress Maurice made in Paris was extraordinarily rapid. His academic studies contributed little. Formative guidance came from a friend he found at the Académie Julian, the Canadian painter James Wilson Morrice, with whose artistic aims he was very much in sympathy. Striking similarities in their work continued long after their first association. Often they painted the same subject at the same place, even when not there at the same time. Both men have in their work an

10   LADY WITH RED SASH   about 1900

5   One of SEVEN SKETCHES OF PARIS   1893   (23)

element of naïveté and a conscious touch of humor, sometimes achieved by identical devices: for instance, by introducing into pictures amusing minor figures such as a marionette-like pair of red-pantalooned poilus (No. 104, ill. p. 101) or twin Italian soldiers. Morrice, the son of a wealthy Presbyterian merchant from Montreal, was younger than Prendergast but had been in Paris longer. His friends were mostly British: the painters Charles Conder, Walter Sickert and Aubrey Beardsley. They used to gather at the Chat Blanc in Montparnasse with the writers Arnold Bennett and Somerset Maugham, and an Irishman named Roderick O'Connor who was the theorist of the Chat Blanc and knew more about Cézanne and Gauguin than anyone there. In this milieu Morrice was perforce guide and mentor to Prendergast. Yet he also had a lively appreciation of Prendergast's unique gifts. His rooms on the Quai Grands-Augustins, which he occupied from 1898 to 1916, were decorated with a Conder fan, a Picasso sketch, a Modigliani drawing and several water-color studies and sketches by Maurice Prendergast.

The friendship was mutually beneficial. A comparison of their sketchbooks for these years shows an inseparable exchange of motifs, ideas and techniques. Both strove to capture in a sketch the idiosyncrasy of the subject, and both made rapid sketches of children, especially little girls, of women, horses, hansom cabs and, more rarely, of men. Of the two, Prendergast's work has the greater freedom and feeling of improvisation. They also painted water-color studies that filled facing pages of their sketchbooks, and, on especially prepared little panels of wood or cardboard hardly larger than an open hand, they made complete oil paintings. These are more than sketches, better than *pochades*; they are full realizations of an experience. Morrice was credited in Paris with having invented this form. Prendergast's group of seven exquisite little panels at the Addison Gallery in Andover is a classic example of this type (No. 5, ill. p. 23). There were also opportunities for Prendergast to observe the working methods of Morrice's friends. Conder joined him and Morrice on a painting trip to St. Malo and Dinard, and in 1891 and again in 1892 he was painting in Dieppe frequented by many of this group, especially Beardsley and Sickert. After working alone for so many years, this must have been an expansive experience for Maurice Prendergast.

His significance as an artist began in this period in France in the early nineties. His association with Morrice and his circle was crucial and formative. Without it his (25) potentialities might not have been realized. It influenced his choice of subject matter, established his methods of working, and gave a direction to his taste that led him ultimately to an honored place among the early advocates of modern art in America. His painting was at first conditioned by the influences that were then affecting Morrice's painting: Whistler and Manet. This is seen in the early oils, particularly in the beach scenes *Dieppe* (Nos. 3 and 4, ill. p. 135) and *Lady with Red Sash* (No. 10, ill. p. 24). His water colors have a wider orientation showing, in addition, a knowledge of Degas, Toulouse-Lautrec, Japanese prints, and the Nabis: Bonnard, Vuillard, Vallotton and their associates. *Along the Boulevard* (No. 53, ill. p. 141) suggests a specific debt to Pierre Bonnard. The interest in Whistler wanes as his career develops. It is the familiarity with the Post-Impressionists that becomes the decisive element in the formation of his individual style. Though he had expanded his knowledge of media, he chose to work chiefly in water color. Perhaps this practice can only be explained because he could not easily afford oils and canvas. Yet the few oils he did are not adversely affected by economy but are often thickly painted. Whatever the reason for his choice, his work in water color was the more distinguished part of his performance in Paris. He returned to America an accomplished watercolorist where eventually he would be ranked with Winslow Homer and John Marin as American masters of this medium.

During Maurice's absence, his brother Charles had given up selling metal ware and had gone into business for himself in Winchester, not far from Boston, where he made ornamented doors and mantels. He was doing quite well when Maurice returned from Paris, without money and already hard of hearing. This was very probably late in 1894 or early in 1895. Maurice and the Winchester painter Herman Dudley Murphy, who established a frame shop near Copley Square in Boston, persuaded Charles to give up doors and mantels for picture frames. This, fortunately, Charles did and today these frames are almost as much sought after as his decorative, incised gesso panels. Maurice came to live with him in Winchester and from there made painting excursions on the north shore to Beachmont, Marblehead and Revere Beach, and to the South Boston Pier. When not occupied with his painting, he helped Charles make frames.

These water colors done from 1895 to 1898 begin his celebration of the New England holiday scene. His technique continues to be the free, direct manner of his

63   LOW TIDE, BEACHMONT   1897   (27)

Paris water colors; the tonality remains cool, while accents of red and red-violet are much favored. Compositions have become more diffuse. Removed from immediate contact with Parisian sophistication, his native simplicity was reasserting itself. His humor is irrepressible in this period, especially in the work he did at Beachmont. In *Low Tide, Beachmont* (No. 63, ill. p. 27), for instance, the manner in which the women manage their skirts as they move precariously over the rocks is more amusing than graceful. They are like country cousins of the poised little Parisiennes seen in *Paris Boulevard in Rain* (No. 52, ill. p. 140). Figures have pert, doll-like faces; the eyes, nose and mouth sometimes indicated with dots. In many ways the whimsical, fresh naïve quality associated with his artistic character is more vividly present in these water colors than in anything Prendergast painted in France.

Now that he could demonstrate the advantages and enjoy the prestige of foreign study, Boston began to treat him with some consideration. Immediately upon coming home he received a commission to do a hundred and thirty-seven illustrations and page decorations for an edition of Sir James Barrie's *My Lady Nicotine* which was published in Boston in 1896. Though the drawings are not of a consistently high quality, they are always worthy of the work they illustrate. They are in perfect rapport with the ingenuous quality of this particular product of Barrie's demure mind. Much more significant for Maurice's career was the result of an exhibition of his paintings, reputedly held at the Chase Gallery in 1897. It brought his work to the attention of his first patrons, Mr. and Mrs. Montgomery Sears, who under the guidance of their friend, Mary Cassatt, were building a distinguished collection. With help from the Sears Maurice was able to go to Europe again.

ITALY

Maurice spent about a year on his third visit to Europe, from 1898 to 1899. Though he may have visited his old haunts in Paris, and even made a short trip to St. Malo, he certainly spent most of the time in Italy. In Venice Charles was able to join him for a short stay. There, along with the American artist Gedney Bunce, they would spend their afternoons at the Café Oriental where Maurice sketched the holiday crowds and the excursion boats coming in from the Lido. Their evenings were spent with a group of artists at Florian's in sight of the splendor of St. Mark's. All too soon,

66   ST. MARK'S, VENICE   1898   (29)

it was time for Charles to return to America. Shortly after he left, Maurice became seriously ill and underwent two operations at the Cosmopolitan Hospital in Venice where he was detained for two months. From the hospital he wrote to Charles: "It is too bad for your sake that I am sick. It would be so fine to be home in the old studio helping you along with the frames. We together are such a fine team."

Despite his illness, Maurice did a great deal of work in Italy. He painted in Venice for over six months altogether, though these months were not consecutive. In between times he went to see the frescoes at Padua and Florence, and spent two months painting in Siena. From there he visited Orvieto, and then went on to Rome where he painted during the winter of 1898–99. Before going back to Venice he made a brief visit to Naples and Capri. The work he had done in Italy was exhibited at the Chase Gallery in Boston late in 1899, and in January 1900 he and Herman Dudley Murphy had a joint exhibition at the Art Institute in Chicago, where Maurice exhibited fifteen water colors and fifteen monotypes. All the water colors had been done in Italy; one of them in Capri, the majority of them in Venice. This was apparently his first important recognition. The water color *Market Place, Venice* (No. 78, ill. p. 31), in Mrs. Charles Prendergast's collection, is a definitive example of this period. In the sparkling view from the steps of the Rialto are found the formative influences of his career up to this point: the brick structure at the right inspires a striking empathy with his native Faneuil Hall Market in Boston; no less does the composition and foreground figure suggest the influence of the Japanese print; and thirdly, there is the inevitable stimulus of the festive Venetian scene to Prendergast's naturally exuberant spirit.

Italian art was an overwhelming experience for Maurice. He said in Venice: "It makes me ashamed of my own work when I see such glories." Something of his excitement is communicated through his sketchbooks. The records he made of pictures that moved him are hardly sketches at all; just a few lines within an enframement to indicate the main movement of a composition. It is as though the thought of how much there was to see and record inhibited fuller notation. He took time to jot down color notes: "Black and oranges trees" or "Girl, purple drapery, green and orange foreground with animals." On the last page of one book are the words: "Carpaccio Vittore, Veneziana." He had discovered not only one of the most charming painters of the Venetian Renaissance, but also had encountered a taste and talent akin to his

78 MARKET PLACE, VENICE 1898   (31)

own. The thrill of the encounter was still with him twelve years later when he described it to Charles Hovey Pepper.

Like Maurice, Carpaccio loved pageantry and processions. He too had a native gift of mimicry, a quickness in observing and recording expressive aspects of pose and gesture, an unfailing instinct for color, and a fertile inventiveness in decoration. He would enliven a picture with any costume, plant, animal, or impedimenta that amused him. The balloons, parasols, goats, dogs, hobby-horse steeds and hybrid creatures of uncertain zoological antecedent that appear in pictures by Maurice over the years are his expression of an identical taste. Balloons and parasols appear first in his Paris pictures; banners he adopted in Venice. Dogs, swans and indeterminate animals appear more frequently in his late oils which are free creations built on the memories of earlier impressions. Specimens are culled from many sources: from the Persian-like ornament of his brother's gesso panels; from the blue Persian jar decorated with animals in which he himself kept his brushes; possibly from Italian frescoes, perhaps those by Benozzo Gozzoli; and certainly the wonderously colored dogs of Carpaccio are remembered. The immediate effect of Carpaccio's example was to encourage Maurice in following his natural bent. In his first Venetian series of water colors he declares his artistic maturity.

In Italy he must have worked mainly in water color, and to a lesser degree in monotype. Except for *Ponte della Paglia* (No. 9, ill. p. 33), which was probably painted in America from a water color done in Venice, few oils from this visit are at present known. Primarily, Venice affected his use of color: it becomes warmer and richer than the delicate, cool harmonies of his Paris work. Carpaccio's *Saint Ursula* series offered him many suggestions for composition and stimulated an interest in subjects involving crowds, processions, festivals, and all scenes that brought into play a spotted pattern of bright accents of color. The work done in Italy has a sense of palpability, something akin to monumentality, with less of the feeling of a rapidly recorded, fleeting impression of a remembered moment that was so characteristic of the work he did in Paris. In the Paris pictures a silhouette is achieved with a twist of the brush; in the Venetian work the contour is firmer and the local color does not wander beyond it. In Paris he confined his interest in movement to that of an individual figure or relatively small group; in Italy the tendency is to extend it to include the busy activity of large masses of people. This is supremely demonstrated in the

9 PONTE DELLA PAGLIA 1899   (33)

Boston Museum's water color *Umbrellas in the Rain, Venice* (No. 77, ill. p. 35). The impact of Venice and Italy is not spent in the abundance of work he did there. One senses the echo of old Italian frescoes in the union of fantasy and formality that pervades his late festivals and processions.

BOSTON and NEW YORK

Maurice Prendergast is the leading American exponent of the printed medium of the colored monotype which he developed to its fullest potential. Between 1892 and 1905 he may have produced as many as two hundred monotypes, in addition to his water colors and a limited number of oils. Many of these were printed in Boston; a few were either made in Venice or from remembered impressions of that city; while another large group portray the New England coast, particularly Nahant. He rather cryptically outlined his method of producing them in instructions that he gave to his only pupil, Mrs. Oliver Williams, in 1905: "Paint on copper in oils, wiping parts to be white. When picture suits you, place on it Japanese paper and either press in a press or rub with a spoon till it pleases you. Sometimes the second or third plate is the best." By "plate" he surely meant "print," since he pulled more than one impression from his monotype plates, following the precedent set by Degas who sought softer effects from a second or third impression. Subjects and compositions developed by Maurice in this medium were often used in water colors and oils. Yet he must have considered his monotypes as something more than preparatory studies since he exhibited them on at least three occasions between 1899 and 1901, in Boston, Chicago and Cincinnati. The representations of the Nouveau Cirque in Paris, a subject so reminiscent of Seurat's and Toulouse-Lautrec's interest in the circus, are reserved to the medium of monotype, as is the bold and original composition of the *Orange Market* (No. 133, ill. p. 37).

Though only incidentally a print maker, his monotypes show a remarkable command of the medium. He handles its soft, diffuse effects with great sensitivity. It was particularly suited to the rendering of one of his favorite subjects: street scenes on a wet day. The diffusion of the medium also accents the Whistlerian quality of the color. It is extremely subtle in these prints; juxtaposed reds and violets, delicate pinks, blues, greens and yellows are all fused with misty grays and occasionally strengthened with sharp accents of black. One of two entitled *Primrose Hill* has

(34)

77 UMBRELLAS IN THE RAIN, VENICE 1899 (35)

"London" added in the plate. They may have been done from sketches made during his visit to England in 1886. If so, they become part of the very scant artistic record remaining from that first European venture. It also is possible that he visited London on his second or third trip abroad.

The monotypes of street scenes in Boston find their inspiration in work he did in Paris. *Tremont Street, Boston* (No. 137, ill. p. 153), done around 1902, puts in sharp focus the question of how well he knew the work of Bonnard at this early date. Names of members of the Nabis do not appear in Maurice's sketchbooks until around 1910, yet there were many opportunities for him to know their work before that year. The Nabis were students at the Académie Julian in 1888. The group was formed in 1889, and held its first exhibition in 1891. James W. Morrice, guide and mentor to Prendergast in Paris, had been at the Julian since 1890. Maurice himself was certainly there early in 1892. In March and April of that year the Nabis exhibited at the Salon des Indépendents, and again in November at le Barc de Bouteville. From 1893 to 1899 their work could be seen at the shop of Père Tanguy, at Vollard's and at Durand Ruel's. Maurice visited Paris on his way to or from Italy in 1898–99, and it is possible that he had not yet returned to America in 1895 when Vollard published twelve lithographs by Bonnard under the title *Quelques aspects de la vie de Paris.* One of these lithographs, *Rue le soir sous la pluie,* is clearly the prototype of Maurice's monotype *Tremont Street, Boston* (No. 137, ill. p. 153). Differences in composition are slight, in color, somewhat greater; subject and elements represented are identical. There are also suggestions from the Bonnard suite in some of the water colors Maurice did of Central Park. Indeed, these New York pictures and the monotypes of Boston street scenes could be thought of as series on each city.

After his return from Italy in 1899, Maurice's reputation began to develop quietly. A few discriminating people in Boston, such as Mr. and Mrs. Montgomery Sears, were buying his work steadily, and exhibitions were making him known elsewhere. In 1901 he received a bronze medal for the water color *The Stony Beach* (No. 86, ill. p. 129), exhibited at the Pan-American Exposition in Buffalo, and in 1905 he had an exhibition at the Macbeth Gallery in New York. His life apart from painting during these years was relatively uneventful. He spent part of his time helping Charles make frames. Because of Charles' gregariousness the workshop in Winchester was frequently filled with visitors. When Maurice found this too distract-

133 ORANGE MARKET about 1899 (37)

ing he would move back to Boston. For several years before 1905 he had a small room on Huntington Avenue, and here most of his monotypes were made. From there he moved to 65 Pickering Street. He also wanted to be in Boston for reasons of health, since his deafness was becoming much worse. Without consulting a doctor, he undertook a self-devised program of physical conditioning in the hope that better general health would improve his hearing. It involved sun bathing and swimming on L Street beach in South Boston, no matter what the weather. In 1905, when he was forty-six, he swam there as early as March and as late as November. His hearing did not improve.

Sometime between 1905 and 1908 both brothers decided to live in Boston permanently. Before leaving Winchester they made a bonfire of much of the contents of their workshop there and took with them to Boston only a few treasured possessions. It is quite possible that much of Maurice's very early and tentative work went into this fire. At 56 Mount Vernon Street they converted a one-room building that had been a fish market into a studio which remained their home for many years. It was at this address that Max Weber visited Maurice in 1913. Though far from affluent, they were happy in the established pattern of their lives. A comfortable place for working and sleeping, good food, an occasional bottle of wine, and later when living in New York, the price of a dinner at Mouquin's on Sixth Avenue, "a real Paris place" where many of The Eight used to go, was their idea of the good life. Charles' comment on it was: "Nobody had as much fun as Monny and me."

From 1900 to 1909 water color was still the medium favored by Maurice. He painted a great deal in Boston and on the North Shore; in Nahant in 1903 and 1904, and intermittently at Salem Willows from 1904 on. Starting in 1900 and continuing into 1902, he repeatedly went to New York to paint. During these visits he established his long friendship with William Glackens, and perhaps through Glackens came to the attention of Dr. Albert C. Barnes. He also got to know the other artists who would eventually make up The Eight, those who were to be referred to as the "Ash Can School." Of the score or more pictures that he painted in New York, only The East River (No. 92, ill. p. 39) suggests some slight interest in the kind of subject that was attracting Henri, Sloan and Luks. But even here the commonplace is transformed by the lyric magic of his brush. His taste for the color and movement of a holiday scene, for the aimless animation of idling crowds, drew him inevitably

to the park. For many of his admirers his Central Park series rank with his first Venetian series as a high point in his career. These Central Park pictures are a sustained demonstration of his artistic maturity, and of his control of his medium. In them he commands all that he had learned in Europe and subjects it to the service of his unique vision. For compositions he calls upon both his Italian and French experiences. The light, cool tonalities are Impressionist, but not the technique. In addition to their artistic worth, these pictures are an invaluable record of the idle summer days in Central Park at the turn of the century. There is in the extravagantly dressed crowds of women and children an intangible fusion of grace and wit, of elegance and humor. These water colors, along with others painted in the first five years of the century, seemed to sum up the more representational, the nineteenth century phase of his art.

In the decade from 1899, when he returned from Italy, to 1909, when he again went to France, Maurice simultaneously consolidated past gains and developed toward a less representational mode of painting. In water color he adapted ideas and compositions developed abroad to new situations and settings. In his use of oils he began to move toward the unique style he was to achieve in that medium. It has been said that he could not afford to paint in oil until around 1910; yet in 1908 he certainly exhibited a number of oils at the Macbeth Gallery with The Eight. When in 1905 he finally delivered *Salem Willows* (No. 12, ill. p. 114) to Mrs. Oliver Williams, he had been retouching it in his studio for over a year. It is signed and dated 1904. This painting, of course, is quite apart from the small oils he did in France in 1892 and 1893. The indications are that he began to take a serious interest in the medium around 1903 or 1904, and devoted progressively more and more time to it thereafter. It is not surprising, therefore, that Charles Hovey Pepper should have discovered a considerable number of oils in Maurice's studio in 1910, and had photographs made of several. Not all of them can now be accounted for.

Prendergast painted his oils almost entirely in the studio. Subjects and compositions are frequently transcribed from water colors done out-of-doors. Yet, there is never an attempt to recreate the effect of the original water color. The related oil is always a new creation; in it he evolves new variants of his color principle and strives for effects only possible in oil paint. He worked on a very loosely stretched canvas, mixing little or no liquid medium with his paint. The loose canvas drew the

88   MAY DAY, CENTRAL PARK   1901   (41)

heavy paint from the brush somewhat irregularly. The individual quality of his touch and the spongy softness of so many of his surfaces is due in a large measure to this practice. He worked by trial and error, reworking canvases endlessly, yet he was rarely satisfied with the result. Several pictures were in progress simultaneously. Indeed, it is hardly an exaggeration to say that anything that was in his studio was in progress. On one occasion a visitor admired a picture he saw in the studio and returned a few days later to buy it. In the absence of his brother, Charles said to the disappointed buyer: "Yes, I know the picture you have in mind. I thought it one of Maurice's best. But it no longer exists. He began painting on it again, and it just disappeared." Under these circumstances, dating Maurice's undated oils is a hazardous procedure. *Central Park in 1903,* in the Metropolitan Museum, New York, for instance, shows internal evidence of having been worked on as late as 1915.

The pictures Maurice himself dated offer a clue to the evolution of his style and technique. About 1904, when he was beginning to be seriously interested in oil painting, he used a heavy impasto consistently, but varied the brush stroke to suit the object represented: a twirl of a full brush for a parasol, a few broad strokes within a contour line for a female figure. Only in representing foliage is Impressionist divisionism used. Though certainly familiar with the then well-established conventions of Impressionism, he was using them selectively, with freedom, and even license. Essentially, his color system at this time is a pattern of accents against a less intense ground. By 1907 he had moved much farther toward a more abstract style. The brush stroke now performs a decorative function and is less clearly related to the structure of the object defined. The distinction between figure and ground is hazier; both function nearly equally in the over-all pattern rather than the figures alone being a pattern set against a ground color. Since, along with a close value range, the backgrounds and figures were being rendered with equally emphatic brush strokes, the problem of defining contours was acute. This he solved with contour lines of contrasting hues. They added immeasurably to the intricacy of his designs. The demands of representation were giving way before his delight in improvising patterns of color, line and movement. It was painting of this kind that inspired the critics in 1908 to write with pejorative intent such vivid descriptions as "whirling arabesques that tax the eye" and "a jumble of riotous pigment such as one does not see elsewhere."

(42)

91   THE MALL, CENTRAL PARK   1901   (43)

Maurice was first exposed to the critics' wrath when he exhibited in New York in 1908 as one of The Eight. He showed sixteen pieces, eight of which referred back to St. Malo where he had gone from Paris to paint during his student years, and possibly again when he visited Italy in 1898–99. They were, however, recent pictures: the oil paintings he had been developing in his Boston studio from water colors and sketches done abroad years earlier. The reaction to them made it clear that in creating an original style he had moved beyond the reach of contemporary American taste. The Bostonians remained tolerantly amused and patronizing, but the New York critics resorted to invective: "artistic tommy-rot, unadulterated slop, the show would be better if it were that of The Seven rather than The Eight." The St. Malo pictures infuriated them: "... an explosion in a color factory... the product of much cider drunk at St. Malo." But neither damnation by faint praise nor unrestrained abuse induced Maurice to wait upon the delayed understanding of his detractors. With undiminished confidence he went on to discover new means of presenting even rarer harmonies and more extraordinary patterns for the delight of unprejudiced eyes.

EUROPE and NEW DIRECTIONS

After a decade of working independently, Maurice felt a need for renewed contact with the sources of his early inspiration. His fourth and fifth visits to Europe have something of the character of a sentimental journey; they follow the pattern set in the eigthteen nineties. The longer visit was to France in 1909–10 and the shorter to Italy in 1911–12. In France he painted briefly in Paris and for a longer period at St. Malo and Dinard. In Italy he painted chiefly in Venice where again his brother was with him. Charles was in Italy to study Renaissance picture frames, but he must also have looked closely at incised gesso panels for his work of this type starts in 1912. Between the two visits, in March 1911, Maurice shared an exhibition with Charles Hopkinson and Charles Hovey Pepper at the Copley Gallery in Boston where he showed five oils of subjects in or near that city. This was his last exhibition in Boston during his lifetime. By the summer of 1912 he had returned from Italy and was on a painting tour in the Berkshires and New Hampshire. Other events in 1912 indicate that he was keeping in close touch with his friends in New York and making new

14 SUMMER IN THE PARK 1905–07 **(45)**

ones there. He went with Arthur B. Davies to Max Weber's studio on 14th Street to select a picture for a group show at the New York Union League Club in which he and Davies were also participating, and he exhibited, too, at the Cosmopolitan Club in New York that year. He was asked to join the Association of American Painters and Sculptors Incorporated and as a member took part in February and March 1913 in the International Exhibition of Modern Art which has come to be known as the Armory Show. His seven water colors were among the most "advanced" works shown by an American artist on this historic occasion. In the ensuing rout William Glackens tried to calm the frenzied critics by reminding them that Maurice had for years been "making patterns of joyous color" and that he was "one of the men who has been consistently and thoroughly modern."

Renewed contact with French art in 1909–10 stimulated a period of intense experimentation in Maurice's career that lasted for nearly five years. During these years he not only experimented with new techniques, but also with new subject matter. He made complete studies of the female nude, introduced this motif into his marine and pastoral idyls, painted portraits, did a number of still-life studies, and explored new potentialities of mood in his favorite theme of people seeking recreation out-of-doors. When this period of diversification was over, these out-of-door subjects, treated in mural-like compositions, again became his chief preoccupation, but he now brought to them a new and greater subtlety of means and of feeling.

Technically the water colors done at St. Malo around 1910 differ noticeably from earlier work done in this medium. The drawing has become almost playful, value contrasts are sharper, color is more brilliant, more frequently broken, and in some passages is applied in rectangular strokes that form a mosaic. These passages strongly suggest the technique evolved by Signac from Seurat's theories. The mosaic effect is more consistent in the few oils Maurice did on St. Malo themes, but it never falls into the pedantry of a system. His intuitive reinterpretation of Signac's style reaches its boldest expression in the *Promenade* (No. 34, ill. p. 122), one of two mural-scale panels painted for John Quinn in 1914–15. There the mosaic effect is an integral part of the design and the component rectangular strokes are scaled to the large dimensions of the picture. These suggestions from Signac play an active part in Maurice's final style. He used them freely, however, ignoring their theoretical

19 SEASHORE 1910 (47)

justification. There are in his St. Malo sketchbooks sketches rendered in circles of varying sizes very like the round spots of color seen in his later paintings. Since no color notes accompany the circles, it appears that he was interested in their possibilities as pattern and texture. In his late pictures rectangular strokes and round spots are combined, both rendered with his characteristic softness. This fusion transforms the mosaic effect into his own unique "tapestried" surface.

In this five-year period Maurice also experimented with media, and again there were lasting results. He had done some work in pastel between 1898 and 1905 and then took up the medium again in 1912, using it intermittently until 1919. In France in 1909–10 he started to combine pastel with water color and opaque Chinese white. These mixed media he used with greater frequency in the next ten years than pastel alone. Work of this type done in Paris is somewhat grayer than the pure water colors, but eventually he used the combination to produce a suffused, bright, almost shadowless radiance, a luminous effect that makes of color not a record of light but its source. This is an effect that often accompanies the tapestried surface of his late oils.

The work done in Venice in 1911–12 is a further step away from the representational character of his early work. Though the color is not quite as brilliant, the technique is as free as it was in the recent St. Malo water colors. There is perhaps an even greater freedom in the manipulation of scale within a composition; sizes of figures are determined by the exigencies of design, not of representation. His favored medium was water color, though a few pieces have pastel added. On this visit he seems to have been especially attracted to the bridges of Venice; he did several versions of each one that took his fancy, exploring all its pictorial possibilities. A glance from the second Venetian series back to the first would indicate how far toward twentieth century painting he had moved.

Between 1910 and 1912 Maurice painted a few portraits of unidentified subjects. His experience as a portrait painter was limited. In 1902 he had successfully completed a full-length group portrait of Mrs. Oliver Williams, her baby son and his nurse (No. 11, ill. p. 113), and left unfinished a portrait of Miss Annie Jewett, also full-length. The portrait of an *Italian Girl* (No. 23, ill. p. 116) in the collection of Mrs. Charles Prendergast was presumably painted in Venice during his second visit. The other known 1910–12 portraits are all half-length: most of them are of children,

20　GIRL IN BLUE　1910–12　　　　　　　　　　　　(49)

the others of young women. In none of them is the individuality of the sitter stressed. What he caught most successfully was the intent gaze and sweet solemnity of childhood. *Portrait of a Boy* (No. 21, ill. p. 136), now in the Nelson Gallery in Kansas City, is his best effort in this field.

Obviously still concerned with broadening the scope of his painting, Maurice in 1913 started working on flower studies and still lifes of potted plants and fruit. Due to his habit of reworking canvases, some of them were still in progress as late as 1917. For stylistic reasons, these still lifes bring up the question of his knowledge of Cézanne. Practically every critic who has mentioned Maurice has said that he was the first American artist to appreciate the importance of Cézanne. He probably first heard of him from O'Connor, "the theorist of the Chat Blanc," and possibly first saw his work either at Vollard's in 1898, where it had been for sale since the exhibition in 1895, or at the Salon des Indépendants in 1899 where Cézanne exhibited two still lifes and a landscape. The impact of Maurice's knowledge upon American artists has been described by Walter Pach: "... one needs to hear what the continual references to Cézanne in his conversations meant to Americans who knew him abroad and, later, at home." As late as 1905 John Sloan asked Maurice: "Who is this fellow Cézanne?" The 1913 Armory Show answered the question substantially; it may also have stimulated Maurice to a practical exploration of Cézanne's painting problems. The still lifes that he started that year show an attempt to synthesize line and color for the definition of mass and space, rather than using them primarily for pattern and texture as he had done previously. Clear and handsome examples are the Whitney Museum's *Cinerarias and Fruit* (No. 35, ill. p. 51) and Mrs. Charles Prendergast's *Still Life with Apples* (No. 28, ill. p. 118). Cézanne, however, was essentially a builder who laid bare the structural bones of his pictures. Such austerity was uncongenial to Maurice's talent for fantasy and decoration. This he surely realized, for it is only in these still lifes that he let admiration lead to emulation.

In his search for new directions, Maurice reviewed earlier sources of inspiration. Drouet's gallery in Paris is noted in the sketchbooks he used between 1909 and 1912. Bonnard, Vuillard, Vallotton and K. X. Roussel exhibited there so frequently that they were known as the Drouet group. On another page K. X. Roussel's name appears along with that of Maurice Denis. Both these men admired Gauguin and

35 CINERARIAS AND FRUIT 1915 (51)

were influenced by his color and the decorative aspects of his style. Roussel favored open-air subjects and motifs drawn from mythology, rendering them with a heavy impasto and softness of touch very like Maurice Prendergast's own. Maurice, too, began to consult mythology about this time. He transcribed from the *Dionisiaca* into his sketchbook an entire poem by Nonos, lines of which read:

"Under the green boughs the wood nymph reclining
Hears the voice of the sea nymph in love songs repining."

Though Maurice in no sense inclined to the literary, he does in his later work frequently equate contemporary girls on holiday with "nymphs" of both the wood and sea variety; that is, if one can so interpret clothed and nude girls, seemingly unconscious of each other, idling together in settings that combine trees and sea. *The Picnic* at the National Gallery, Ottawa, from around 1915, is a fascinating example.

This interest in pagan mythology makes its contribution to his exploration of mood. *Castle Island,* painted in 1912, is literally the darkest picture he ever painted. It invades areas of mood and emotion entirely alien to the rest of his work. In it he usual counterpoint of gaiety and wistfulness almost becomes one of innocence and violence. Superficially, the subject is his very frequent one of people idling under trees near rocks and water, but acidulous blue-greens and dark violet opposed to glowing pinks and sulphurous moonlight green, produce an ominous mood. The figures seem unconscious of the threatening atmosphere, and quite unaware of a tiny, satyr-like silhouette prancing atop a rock near the center. It provides the final note of sinister implication.

John Quinn liked Maurice's unusual efforts; perhaps they were stimulated by his patronage, as in the case of the mural-scale panels. His collection included, in addition to the panels, a nude figure study in oil called *Waterfall* (No. 22, ill. p. 136) and the water color *The Bathers* (No. 114, ill. p. 149). There is also an unusual oil done in 1913, *Bathers by a Waterfall,* in the collection of Miss Adelaide M. De Groot. Here Maurice set aside Signac's Neo-Impressionism and mosaic effects to work technically in a manner closer to Roussel's. The rendering of the blue water areas is so broad that he picture was once mistakenly called *The Beach.* However, the picture as a whole suggests more than a casual debt to Gauguin. The most

37   THE COVE   1916   (53)

independent and successful work of this genre is Mrs. Charles Prendergast's *Eight Bathers* (No. 38, ill. p. 14).

The years from 1909 to 1914 had been in many ways a time of crisis for Maurice. He was past fifty and almost completely deaf. For twenty years or more he had given all his time to painting, yet his great effort and singular talent had won him relatively little recognition. Only a few understood and appreciated his work. For the first time his gentleness and humor show signs of strain. His sketchbooks for the period are filled with the most violent outbursts of Nietzsche. The visits to Europe were as unsettling as they were stimulating. So much had happened in the years he had been away from there. Actually, the work he had been doing independently in Boston had developed in much the same direction as that taken by the younger Post-Impressionists. Nevertheless, for a while after his return to America he seems to have been unsure of his way, and consequently followed where others led. A few of the new directions were for him dead ends. The renewed contact with the Post-Impressionists was the most fruitful, particularly his interest in Signac and Roussel. Finally, his determination to be himself reasserted itself. He retained from this complex period of extensive exploration only what would serve his unique vision.

THE LAST DECADE

Maurice's departure from Boston in 1914 breaks an established rhythm in his life and career. The alternating pattern of short periods of discovery and inspiration in Europe and long periods of adaption and integration at home comes to an end. Miss Lillie Bliss and John Quinn sponsored that year his sixth and last trip to Europe, but it was cut short by the first World War and little or no painting was done. Though the quality of his art was far from being widely recognized in Boston, a few artists and patrons there had for years given him both encouragement and practical help. They failed, however, to overcome his feeling that Boston was not the most advantageous place for him. He felt out of sympathy with the prevailing attitude toward artists, and had once there been asked to leave a restaurant because he was sketching some young ladies at a nearby table. He must have wished for a more permissive environment. The growing number and closeness of his friendships in New York, plus the significance of the recent Armory Show, fixed his determina-

111 THE RIDER   about 1914   (55)

tion to move there. As always, Charles made it possible. He obtained an unusually large order for frames from a Philadelphia insurance company for portraits of past presidents. On the strength of it the brothers quit Boston and moved to a studio on the top floor of a building at 50 South Washington Square, New York. Occupying a studio on a lower floor of the same building was their old friend William Glackens.

In May 1915 the large panels John Quinn had commissioned Maurice, Walt Kuhn and Arthur B. Davies to do were shown at the Montross Gallery along with one of Charles Prendergast's incised gesso panels. Glackens and Sheeler were also represented in this exhibition. That same year Maurice exhibited at the Brummer Gallery, and in March 1917 he shared an exhibition at the Bourgeois Gallery with Glackens again and John Marin. Maurice was now at the scene of the revolution fomenting in American art. Much of it was for him a familiar story: he had for years been "consistently . . . modern."

The decade he spent in New York is the quiet evening of his career. He was near his friends, his worst financial difficulties were past, and the doubts that had in recent years led to such intensive experimentation in his work were now calmed. He had found his way again. He spent his days integrating on canvas, not only his recently acquired knowledge, but the painting experiences of a lifetime. During the winter months of this last decade he painted daily in his studio on Washington Square. In the summers he went to his beloved New England coast to do water colors out-of-doors. He reverted to a pattern of work that had been established when he first started painting in oil. On a trip to the coast or elsewhere, he would make a number of water colors of a holiday scene that struck his fancy; back in the studio the design possibilities of this scene would be explored in compositions in oil. The idea would be reworked in several versions with considerable variety. This would continue until he made another trip, and a new locale and set of figures would become the point of departure for a fresh series of designs. In his late oils, however, there is an important difference: older memories are interwoven with recent impressions. These pictures truly have the character of poetry. They are the products of emotion recollected in tranquility.

It is difficult to ascertain where in particular on the New England coast he painted each summer of this decade. A letter reveals that he was in Annisquam in 1915. Sketchbooks and titled water colors indicate repeated visits to Gloucester, Ipswich,

43   ON THE BEACH, No. 3   1918   (57)

Lanesville, Marblehead, Nahant, Rockport, Salem Willows and Swampscott. Most of the pictures related to Nahant and Swampscott were done in 1916 and 1917; those related to Salem Willows in 1918 and 1919. There are two groups of Gloucester water colors; one from 1915 and the other from 1919 and 1920. He seems to have been painting in Marblehead as late as 1922.

In 1918 there is a marked change in his water colors. The brushwork becomes extremely free and broad, and representation quite summary. Color begins to take on a new intensity. By 1919 some of his water colors are keyed to a pure red and maintain a consistently high intensity throughout. They have an almost Matisse-like brilliance and an expressionistic intensity, as strikingly, exemplified by the *Four Girls in Meadow* (No. 122, ill. p. 59) in Mrs. Charles Prendergast's collection. Though in oil painting he continued to use the pale tonalities of Impressionism to the very end, this interest in greater brilliance did affect *Sunday Promenade* (No. 48, ill. p. 123), an oil dating from 1922. There the color progressively increases in intensity toward the center of the picture where it culminates in a brilliant red-orange. A new restraint in the use of white contributes to the resonance. From the augmented brilliance of these very late water colors, and from such a picture as *Sunday Promenade,* it is evident that at the end of his career Maurice was about to take another step forward in a long and consistent development.

Changes in his oil painting during this last decade are somewhat more gradual. From 1913 forward figures tend to become larger in scale, and in some pictures they have the distinctly mannerist proportions of small heads and tall, slender bodies. Color and brushwork synthesize innovations he had been developing for years. *Figures in a Park* (No. 30, ill. p. 119), painted in 1914, is the most consistently "pointillist" picture he ever painted, but the spots of color are considerably larger than either Seurat's or Signac's. *The Swans* (No. 39, ill. p. 138), worked on from 1916 to 1918, has a fully synthesized, tapestried surface; its color is magical. From a distance of fifteen feet the picture takes on an exquisitely delicate, pale green tonality behind which the warmer tones seem to fluctuate. Surely, no one up to that time had used color in quite that way. *Acadia* in the Museum of Modern Art, done in 1922 and probably the last important oil he painted, has a similar surface, but the color is warmer and a little nearer the brillant intensity of *Sunday Promenade,* done the same year.

122   FOUR GIRLS IN MEADOW   about 1919-20   (59)

The similar subject matter of so many pictures by Maurice, his almost undeviating allegiance to the simple theme of people at leisure in the out-of-doors, has too often obscured both the originality of his innovations and the significance of his aesthetic achievement. An explanation of the iconography of almost any one of the oils he painted in his studio in New York would require an unravelling of all the experiences that stimulated his painting throughout his life. Fact and fantasy, the recent and the distant past, America and Europe are all woven together in these summations. In a timeless land of undifferentiated memories, horsemen and schooners, goats, swans and dogs, Eton-collared boys on donkeys, half-clothed girls and New England cottages, flowers, fans, wagons, paddle-boats and parasols, all take their place with serene inevitability. The magic of his art has banished incongruity, and all the happy holidays by all the seas and in all the parks can now go on simultaneously forever.

— —

In 1922 Maurice's health began to fail. He did not go to New England in 1923. That year the Corcoran Gallery in Washington awarded him the third William A. Clark Prize and the Corcoran Bronze Medal. He was bedridden at the time. He died in New York on the first of February 1924.

46   PICNIC GROVE   about 1918   (61)

Chronology

MAURICE BRAZIL PRENDERGAST

1859–1924

1859
Born October 10 in St. John's, Newfoundland.

1861
Family moves to Boston, Massachusetts.

1873
Graduates from Rice Grammar School, Boston. Goes to work for the dry goods firm of Loring and Waterhouse.

1883
Earns his living lettering show cards. His apprenticeship has been completed for some time.

1886
First trip abroad, to England on a cattle boat. Probably went to Paris for a short stay.

1887
Sketching in Everett, Massachusetts in May.

1889
Painting at Rockport, Maine for a few weeks in the summer.

1891
Second trip abroad. Studies in Paris at the Académie Julian with Jean Paul Laurens and Blanc, and at the Colarossi School. Summer

trips to Dieppe in 1892, to St. Malo and Dinard until 1894.

1893
Sketches published in The Studio in London.

1894–95
Returns to America. Chief residence Winchester, Massachusetts until 1905.

1896
Illustrated edition of Barrie's *My Lady Nicotine,* published in Boston.

1897
Exhibits at the Chase Gallery, Boston. Starts using a studio on Huntington Avenue. Keeps it until 1905 when he moves to 65 Pickering Street.

1898
Third trip abroad: to Italy, Venice chiefly. Brief visits to St. Malo and Paris.

1899
Returns to America. Exhibition at the Chase Gallery, Boston.

1900
Joint exhibition with Herman Dudley Murphy at the Art Institute, Chicago.

1901
Bronze Medal for Water color, Pan-American Exposition, Buffalo, New York. Exhibition of monotypes, Cincinnati Museum. Starts painting water colors in New York.

1903
Painting in Nahant, also in 1904.

1905
Exhibits with Charles Hopkinson and Charles Hovey Pepper at the Kimball Gallery, Boston. Exhibition at Macbeth Gallery, New York. Sometime between 1905 and 1908 moves from

Winchester to a permanent address at 56 Mount Vernon Street, Boston.

1908
Exhibits as one of The Eight in New York, Chicago and Detroit.

1909
Fourth trip abroad: to Paris and St. Malo. Stays until 1910.

1911
Exhibits with Hopkinson and Pepper at the Copley Gallery, Boston. Fifth trip abroad: to Italy. Stays until 1912.

1912
Participates in group exhibition at Union League Club, New York. Exhibits at Cosmopolitan Club, New York. Painting in New Hampshire.

1913
Takes part in the Armory Show.

1914
Sixth and last trip to Europe; very short. Moves to 50 South Washington Square, New York. Paints in New England in the summers until 1922.

1915
Participates in group exhibition at Montross Gallery, New York. Exhibition at the Brummer Gallery, New York.

1917
Exhibits with William Glackens and John Marin at the Bourgeois Gallery, New York.

1923
Third William A. Clark Prize and Corcoran Bronze Medal, Corcoran Gallery of Art, Washington, D. C.

1924
Dies February 1 in New York.

Selected Bibliography

BASSO, HAMILTON. "A Glimpse of Heaven." New Yorker, Vol. 22, July 27, 1946, pp. 24–28; August 3, 1946, pp. 28–32.

BREUNING, MARGARET. *Maurice Prendergast*. New York, Whitney Museum of American Art, 1931 (American Artists Series). 17 pages, 20 illustrations.

BROOKS, VAN WYCK. "Anecdotes of Maurice Prendergast" in *The Prendergasts,* a Retrospective Exhibition, Addison Gallery of American Art, Andover, Massachusetts. Reprinted *Magazine of Art,* October 1938.

BUCHANAN, DONALD W. *James Wilson Morrice,* Toronto, 1936.

MILLIKEN, WILLIAM MATHEWSON. "Maurice Prendergast, American Artist." *The Arts,* Vol. 9, 1926, pp. 181–192.

PACH, WALTER. "Introduction" to *Maurice Prendergast Memorial Exhibition,* Whitney Museum of American Art, New York, February–March, 1934, pp. 5–7.

PEPPER, CHARLES HOVEY. "Is Drawing to Disappear in Artistic Individuality?" *The World Today,* Vol. XIX, No. 1, July 1910, pp. 716–719.

PHILLIPS, DUNCAN. "Maurice Prendergast." *The Arts,* Vol. 5, 1924, pp. 125–131.

SAWYER, CHARLES H. "The Prendergasts." *Parnassus,* October 1938, pp. 9–11.

WELLESLEY COLLEGE, Jewett Arts Center and Museum of Fine Arts, Boston, *4 Boston Masters: Copley, Allston, Prendergast, Bloom;* April–June, 1959 [essays by John McAndrew, Virgil Barker, E. P. Richardson, Hedley H. Rhys and Aline Saarinen].

Catalogue of the Exhibition

Prepared

by

PETER A. WICK

Objects are catalogued chronologically and by medium.

In dimensions height precedes width.

Oils

1 DINARD 1891
Oil on wood panel, 13$^3/_4$ x 10$^1/_4$ inches
Inscribed lower left: *Maurice Prendergast / Dinard / '91*
Lent by Mrs. Charles Prendergast

This little oil was reputedly praised by Laurens with whom Maurice studied at the Académie Julian. Executed in large part with palette knife and thick impasto, it represents the Breton seaport of St. Malo as viewed from Dinard.

2 EVENING SHOWER, PARIS 1892
Oil on wood panel, 12$^1/_2$ x 8$^1/_2$ inches
Signed lower left in yellow: *Prendergast*
Lent by Mr. and Mrs. Perry T. Rathbone

3 DIEPPE 1892
("Red and White Parasols")
Oil on canvas, 13 x 9$^3/_4$ inches
Inscribed lower left: *Prendergast / Dieppe*
Lent by the Whitney Museum of American Art

4 DIEPPE 1892
Oil on canvas, 12 x 9 inches
Inscribed lower left: *Prendergast / Dieppe*
(formerly collection Raymond Chaffetz)
Lent by Mr. and Mrs. Arthur G. Altschul

5 SEVEN SKETCHES IN PARIS 1893
Oil on panel, 6 x 4 inches each
Sined at bottom: *PRENDERGAST*
Lent by the Addison Gallery of American Art, Phillips Academy, Andover

These panels were selected and framed together by Charles Prendergast in 1939 for the Addison Gallery.

16 THE FLYING HORSES about 1908–09   (67)

6   EVENING ON A PLEASURE BOAT (Boston)   about 1894
Oil on canvas, 14 x 22 inches
Signed and inscribed lower left:
   Prendergast: | Evening on a Pleasure Boat
Lent by Mr. and Mrs. John Koch

7   IN THE LIBRARY   about 1895 or 1903–06
Oil on panel, $12^{1}/_{4}$ x $13^{1}/_{2}$ inches
Signed lower right in red: *Prendergast*
Lent by Mrs. Charles Prendergast

8   FRANKLIN PARK (Boston)   1896
Oil on panel, 13 x 16½ inches
Signed and monogrammed lower left: *Prendergast* $\begin{smallmatrix} M \\ B \\ P \end{smallmatrix}$
Lent by Mr. and Mrs. Walter L. Ress

9   PONTE DELLA PAGLIA (Venice)   1899
Oil on canvas, 28 x 23 inches
Signed lower left: *Prendergast*
Lent by the Phillips Collection, Washington

10   LADY WITH RED SASH (Boston)   about 1900
Oil on canvas, 24¼ x 8¼ inches
Signed lower right: *Prendergast*
Lent by Mrs. Charles Prendergast

11   PORTRAIT OF MRS. OLIVER E. WILLIAMS   1902
(with nurse and baby son Oliver)
Oil on canvas, 34 x 24 inches
Signed lower right: *Prendergast*
(acquired directly from the artist)
Lent by Mrs. Oliver E. Williams

12 SALEM WILLOWS   1904
Oil on canvas, 26 x 34 inches
Signed and dated lower right: *Prendergast / 1904*
(acquired directly from the artist)
Lent by Mrs. Oliver E. Williams

Salem Willows was the inspiration for several later versions, notably that in the Newark Museum (about 1918) showing a summer pavilion.
*   The Willows is a marine park in the easterly part of Salem, on a peninsula jutting out on a rugged point. These European white willows were planted by the Salem Board of Health in 1801 to provide a shady walk for convalescents at an old hospital. Nine of the forty trees planted remain.*

13 TUILERIES GARDENS   1904
Oil on canvas, 10 x 14 inches
Signed lower left in red: *Prendergast*
Lent by Mr. and Mrs. Ralph L. Wilson

This and In the Luxembourg Gardens *(No. 15) were painted in the studio after sketches made earlier in Paris.*

14 SUMMER IN THE PARK*   1905–07
Oil on canvas, 15³/₄ x 20¹/₂ inches
Signed lower right in red: *Prendergast*
Lent by the Santa Barbara Museum of Art (Preston Morton Collection)
* Shown only in Boston, San Francisco and Cleveland

15 IN THE LUXEMBOURG GARDENS   1907
Oil on panel, 10½ x 13¾ inches
Signed and dated lower left: *Prendergast / 1907*
(formerly collection Margarett Sargent McKean)
Lent by Mr. and Mrs. Philip F. Newman

Another oil of same dimensions of the Luxembourg Gardens is in a private collection in Cleveland.

16 THE FLYING HORSES about 1908–09
Oil on canvas, $23^7/_8 \times 32^1/_8$ inches
Signed lower right: *Prendergast*
Lent by the Toledo Museum of Art

*This oil is based on the earlier water color of the Merry-Go-Round
in the Springfield Museum. The same subject was painted by Glackens.*

17 PARK BY THE SEA about 1909
Oil on canvas, $10^1/_2 \times 14$ inches
Signed lower right: *Prendergast*
Lent by Mr. and Mrs. Walter Fillin

18 GREEN SHORE 1910
Oil on panel, $9 \times 16^1/_2$ inches
Signed lower right in red: *Prendergast*
Lent anonymously

19 SEASHORE 1910
Oil on canvas, $23^7/_8 \times 32$ inches
Signed lower left of center: *Prendergast*
(formerly collection Adolph Lewisohn)
Lent by the City Art Museum of St. Louis

20 GIRL IN BLUE 1910–12
Oil on canvas, $13^3/_8 \times 11^1/_4$ inches
Signed lower right in red: *Prendergast*
(formerly collection Mrs. William Keighley)
Lent by Joseph H. Hirshhorn

In the Hirshhorn collection is another half-length portrait of a Seated Girl
with clasped hands. Likewise of a similar type is the Girl in Blue Dress *in the
Des Moines Art Center.*

21 PORTRAIT OF A BOY 1910–12
Oil on canvas, 17³/₄ x 14¹/₂ inches
Unsigned
(formerly collection Cornelius J. Sullivan)
Lent by Nelson Gallery – Atkins Museum
   (Gift of Mr. and Mrs. Milton McGreevy through the Westport Fund)

22 WATERFALL 1911
Oil on canvas, 24 x 20 inches
Signed lower left: *Prendergast*
(formerly collections John Quinn, Mrs. John D. Rockefeller, Jr.)
Lent by Dr. and Mrs. Paul Todd Makler

23 ITALIAN GIRL 1911–12
Oil on canvas, 18¹/₂ x 12¹/₄ inches
Signed left below center: *Prendergast*
Lent by Mrs. Charles Prendergast

24 BEACH AT GLOUCESTER 1912–14
Oil on canvas, 31 x 43 inches
Signed lower left of center: *Prendergast*
Lent by Joseph H. Hirshhorn

25 NEW ENGLAND VILLAGE 1912–14
Oil on canvas, 18¹/₄ x 21 inches
Signed lower right in red: *Prendergast*
(formerly collection Mrs. William Steele Gray)
Lent by Mrs. Edward Patterson

26 THE PROMENADE 1913
Oil on canvas, 30 x 34 inches
Signed lower right: *Prendergast*
(formerly collections John Quinn, Alexander M. Bing)
Lent by the Whitney Museum of American Art

(71)

27 LA ROUGE: Portrait of Miss Edith King
("Lady with the Rouge")
Oil on canvas, 28¼ x 31¼ inches
Signed lower left: *Prendergast*
Lent by Lehigh University, Permanent Collection
    (Gift of Mr. and Mrs. Ralph L. Wilson)

Miss King, known by her friends as " La bella Simonetta," was a teacher at the
Buckingham School in Cambridge. Later in New York she and Dorothy Coit,
a fellow teacher, established the King-Coit Theatre for children's productions.
The title of the painting would seem to derive from a story connected with her
sitting for the portrait when it was suggested, perhaps jokingly, that she apply
more color to her cheeks.
    Another portrait, half-length, of Edith King, in the collection of Miss Adelaide
Milton de Groot, shows a young woman wearing a brown dress with white
collar and a large blue hat trimmed with red-violet and yellow flowers with
leaves.

28 STILL LIFE WITH APPLES   about 1913–15
Oil on canvas, 13¾ x 18 inches
Signed lower left: *Prendergast*
Lent by Mrs. Charles Prendergast

29 STILL LIFE WITH APPLES   about 1913–15
Oil on canvas, 15 x 18 inches
Signed lower left in red: *Prendergast*
(formerly collection William F. Laporte)
Lent by Mr. and Mrs. Ralph L. Wilson

Two variant versions with fruit, one broadly painted in light tonality,
are in other private collections. A third appeared in the Anderson Galleries'
sale catalogue of the collection of Mr. and Mrs. Cornelius J. Sullivan,
April–May, 1937, No. 51 (ill.).

45 IN THE PARK 1918-20   (73)

30 FIGURES IN A PARK 1914
Oil on canvas, 58 x 49 inches
Unsigned
Lent by Walter P. Chrysler, Jr.

The most uniformly pointillist, not yet his developed tapestry style,
this marks the beginning of the increased scale of his paintings.

31 THE HARBOR 1914
Oil on canvas, 24 x 30 inches
Signed lower left: *Prendergast*
Lent by Mr. and Mrs. Philip F. Newman

32 POPPIES IN BLUE VASE about 1914
Oil on panel, 13¾ x 10½ inches
Signed lower right: *Prendergast*
Lent anonymously

In the Addison Gallery, Andover, is another important example of this type,
Old Fashioned Flowers *(1914).*

33 NIGHT STUDY OF FLOWERS about 1914
Oil on canvas, 13½ x 10 inches
Signed lower right in red: *Prendergast*
(formerly collections Mrs. Stanley B. Resor, Mrs. William Steele Gray)
Lent by Mr. and Mrs. Henry W. Breyer, Jr.

34 PROMENADE 1914–15
Oil on canvas, 83¾ x 134 inches
Signed lower right: *Prendergast*
(formerly collection John Quinn)
Lent by the Detroit Institute of Arts

Cf. the preparatory study (No. 113). John Quinn
commissioned another large decorative panel called "Picnic,"
lately in the Estate of Arthur F. Egner.

35 CINERARIAS AND FRUIT 1915
Oil on canvas, 21 x 27 inches
Signed lower right of center: *Prendergast*
Lent by the Whitney Museum of American Art

36 SUNSET AND SEA FOG 1915
Oil on canvas, 18 x 29½ inches
Signed lower right: *Prendergast*
(formerly collections Duncan Phillips, Oliver B. James)
Lent by the Butler Institute of American Art, Youngstown

37 THE COVE 1916
Oil on canvas, 28 x 39¾ inches
Unsigned
Lent by the Whitney Museum of American Art

38 EIGHT BATHERS 1916–18
Oil on canvas, 28 x 24 inches
Signed lower center in red: *Prendergast*
Lent by Mrs. Charles Prendergast

39 THE SWANS 1916–18
Oil on canvas, 30 x 43 inches
Signed lower right: *Prendergast*
(formerly collection Duncan Phillips)
Lent by the Addison Gallery of American Art, Phillips Academy, Andover
(Bequest of Lillie P. Bliss)

40 SUNSET about 1917
Oil on canvas, 21 x 32 inches
Signed lower right: *Prendergast*
Lent by Mr. and Mrs. Alan H. Temple

(75)

41 HOLIDAYS 1917–18
Oil on canvas, 30 x 43¼ inches
Signed lower left: *Prendergast*
(formerly collection Duncan Phillips)
Lent by the Minneapolis Institute of Arts

42 EARLY EVENING 1917–20
Oil on panel, 15 x 24 inches
Unsigned
Lent by Dr. and Mrs. Paul Todd Makler

43 ON THE BEACH, No. 3 1918
Oil on canvas, 26 x 33³/₈ inches
Signed lower left: *Prendergast*
Lent by the Cleveland Museum of Art (Hinman B. Hurlbut Collection)

44 PROMENADE, GLOUCESTER about 1918
Oil on canvas, 26 x 34 inches
Signed lower right: *Prendergast*
Lent by the Whitney Museum of American Art

45 IN THE PARK 1918–20
Oil on canvas, 21 x 24 inches
Signed lower left: *Prendergast*
(formerly collection Lillie P. Bliss)
Lent by Mrs. Bliss Parkinson

46 PICNIC GROVE about 1918
Oil on canvas, 18¹/₈ x 27¹/₄ inches
Signed lower center in red: *Prendergast*
Lent by the Museum of Fine Arts, Boston

64 SUMMER OUTING ON THE ROCKS 1897–98

47 EDGE OF THE GROVE 1919
("Rider Against Blue Hills")
Oil on canvas, 17½ x 21 inches
Signed lower right: *Prendergast*
Lent by Mrs. Charles Prendergast

48 SUNDAY PROMENADE 1922
Oil on canvas, 23½ x 31¾ inches
Signed lower left: *Prendergast*
(formerly collection Mrs. Walter Ross)
Lent by Mr. and Mrs. M. P. Potamkin

Water Colors and Pastels

49 COTTAGE LANDSCAPE, HAWARDEN (Wales) 1886
Pencil and water color, 11½ x 15¾ inches
Signed lower left in ink: *M. B. Prendergast* / Aug. '86 / Hawarden
Lent by Mr. and Mrs. John G. Pierce

50 OLD WOMAN, PARIS 1891
Water color, 10⅝ x 9⅜ inches
Signed and inscribed upper left and right in ink:
    Prendergast   Paris / *Jan.* / *91*
Lent by Mrs. Charles Prendergast

*This academic study from life, still in the dark manner of the few water colors
of the eighties, is his earliest surviving Paris work. It may have been product of
the Colarossi studio under Courtois. The dated inscription establishes the time
of Prendergast's arrival in Paris on his second European trip.*   (77)

51 LADY ON A WET DAY (Paris)   about 1892
Pencil and water color, 11³/₈ x 8 inches
Signed lower right in ink: *Prendergast*
(formerly collection James Wilson Morrice)
Lent by Mrs. John F. Kraushaar

52 PARIS BOULEVARD IN RAIN   1893
("Champs-Elysées;" "Wet Day, Paris")
Pencil and water color, 12 x 9½ inches
Signed and inscribed lower right in ink:
    To Mable Pelletier / souvenir /
    Maurice B. Prendergast / Paris 93
Lent by Mr. and Mrs. William Marshall Fuller
A preparatory pencil study appears in a Paris sketchbook of 1893–94.

A little water color of the previous year in a private collection,
Paris Street Scene (perhaps the Boulevard des Italiens),
is inscribed "à M. Lichtenstein / souvenier affectueux / M. Brazil Prendergast /
Paris '92." The style is suggestive of Raffaelli.

53 ALONG THE BOULEVARD (Paris)   about 1894
Pencil and water color, 9³/₈ x 12¹/₈ inches
Signed lower left in pen: *Prendergast*
Lent by the Albright Art Gallery, Buffalo

54 CORRIDORS   about 1894
Pencil, pen, with green and gray wash, 6½ x 6¾ inches
Signed lower right in ink: *Prendergast*
(formerly collection James Wilson Morrice)
Lent by Mr. and Mrs. John G. Pierce

There is an unusual fantasy about this wash drawing which isolates it in the
work of Prendergast. The architecture, like a great law court foyer populated
with circulating men, suggests a memory image perhaps inspired by one of   (79)

the subterranean vaulted chambers in the Palais de Justice, Paris (i. e. Salle des Gens d'Armes of Philippe-le-Bel). The drawing has a strange lack of emotional content.

55 WOMAN ARRANGING HER HAIR   about 1894-95
Pencil, pen and water color, 10¼ x 6¼ inches
Signed upper right in ink: *Prendergast*
(formerly collection James Wilson Morrice)
Lent by Mr. and Mrs. John G. Pierce

56 FRANKLIN PARK (Boston)   1894
Pencil and water color, 11 x 19½ inches
Signed lower right: *Prendergast*
(formerly collections Mrs. Montgomery Sears,
    Mrs. J. D. Cameron Bradley)
Lent anonymously

57 SOUTH BOSTON PIER: SUNSET   1895
Pastel, 20½ x 26¼ inches
Signed and dated lower left in pencil: *Prendergast / 95*
Lent by Mr. and Mrs. Donald G. Crowell

58 SOUTH BOSTON PIER   1896
Pencil and water color, 18½ x 13½ inches
Signed lower left in ink: *Maurice B. Prendergast*
Lent by Smith College Museum of Art, Northampton

The pleasure pier at City Point in South Boston was a popular promenade of its day. By taking position at the end of the pier, Prendergast caught its sinuous curve and picturesque shoreline beyond.

59 REVERE BEACH   1896
Pencil and water color, 13⅝ x 9⅞ inches
Signed and dated lower right and left in ink:
    Maurice B. Prendergast / 1896   *Prendergast*
Lent by the City Art Museum of St. Louis

68 PIAZZA DI SAN MARCO 1898-99   (81)

60   REVERE BEACH   about 1896
Water color, 9½ x 12 inches
Signed lower right in ink: *Maurice B. Prendergast*
Lent by Mr. and Mrs. Arthur G. Altschul

61   FLOAT AT LOW TIDE, REVERE BEACH   about 1896
Pencil and water color, 13¼ x 9⅜ inches
Signed lower right in ink: *Maurice B. Prendergast*
Lent by the Addison Gallery of American Art, Phillips Academy, Andover
(Gift of Mrs. William Crowninshield Endicott)

*On his return from Paris Prendergast made frequent excursions to this public
beach just north Boston. If some of these water colors recall Boudin, others
ripple with the fluid shimmer of Whistlers' Venetian studies.*

62   HANDKERCHIEF POINT   1897
Pencil and water color, 20 x 13¾ inches
Signed lower right in pencil: *Prendergast*
Lent by the Museum of Fine Arts, Boston (Gift of Francis W. Fabyan in memory
of Edith Westcott Fabyan)

63   LOW TIDE, BEACHMONT   1897
Pencil and water color, 19½ x 22⅛ inches
Signed and dated lower right in red: *Prendergast / 1897*
Lent by the Worcester Art Museum

*This large study formerly hung in the guest room of Charles Prendergast's home
in Westport and was acquired directly from him. A similar water color, entitled*
Beachmont *(19 x 13 inches), is in the Art Museum of the New Britain Institute,
Conn.*

64   SUMMER OUTING ON THE ROCKS (Nantasket)   1897
Pencil and water color, 15½ x 22 inches
Signed lower left in ink: *Prendergast*
(82)   Lent anonymously

70   CAMPO SANTA MARIA FORMOSA, VENICE   1898   (83)

65 THE LAGOON, VENICE 1898
Pencil and water color, $11\frac{1}{8}$ x $15\frac{3}{8}$ inches
Signed and dated lower right in ink: *Maurice Prendergast 1898*
Lent by the Museum of Modern Art
    (acquired through the Lillie P. Bliss Bequest)

66 ST. MARK'S, VENICE 1898
Pencil and water color, 13 x $18\frac{7}{8}$ inches
Signed lower left in ink: *Prendergast 1898*
Lent by Mrs. Charles Prendergast

A variant, dated 1898, is in a private collection, Boston.

67 EASTER PROCESSION, ST. MARK'S (Venice)   about 1898
Pencil and water color, 18 x 14 inches
Signed lower right in ink: *Maurice B. Prendergast*
(formerly collection Morris Crawford, Sr.)
Lent by Mr. and Mrs. Walter Ross

68 PIAZZA DI SAN MARCO (Venice) 1898–99
Pencil and water color, $16\frac{1}{8}$ x 15 inches
Signed lower left in pencil: *Prendergast*
Lent by the Metropolitan Museum of Art
    (Gift of the Estate of Mrs. Edward Robinson, 1952)

69 RIVA SAN BIAGIO (Venice) 1898
Pencil and water color, 12 x $10\frac{1}{2}$ inches
Signed lower left in pencil: *Riva / San Biagio / Prendergast*
Lent by Oliver Williams

The steamboat ferry (vaporetto) is making a landing at the Riva San Biagio
on the Bacino, just below the Riva degli Schiavoni, and one stop above the
Giardini.

70 · CAMPO SANTA MARIA FORMOSA, VENICE   1898
Water color, 12¾ x 18½ inches
Signed lower left in ink: *Maurice Prendergast*
(formerly collection Henry Sheafer)
Lent by Mr. and Mrs. Arthur G. Altschul

71   FESTIVAL NIGHT, VENICE   1898–99
Water color, 11 x 15 inches
Signed lower right with brush: *Prendergast*
Lent by Mr. and Mrs. Charles C. Cunningham

Prendergast made a mosaic of this subject.

72   GONDOLAS, VENICE   1898
Water color and ink wash, unfinished, 10½ x 14½ inches
Signed lower right with brush: *Prendergast*
Lent by Mrs. William Hayes Bender, Jr.

73   A BRIDGE IN VENICE   1898
Pencil and water color, 11⅛ x 14⅞ inches
Signed lower right in ink: *Maurice B. Prendergast*
Lent by the Cleveland Museum of Art
    (Mr. and Mrs. Edward Belden Greene Memorial)

74   PINCIAN HILL (Rome)   1898
Pencil and water color, 21 x 27 inches
Inscribed lower right: *Pincian Hill / Rome 1898 / Prendergast*
Lent by the Phillips Collection, Washington

75   SPANISH STEPS, ROME   1898
Pencil and water color, unfinished, 20 x 14 inches
Unsigned
Lent by Mr. and Mrs. Roy R. Neuberger

74 PINCIAN HILL 1898

This drawing, like Mulberry Bend Park *(No. 94), apparently unfinished, reveals the pencil tracery in the white areas faintly defining the figures to be added after the background had been washed in. Often, however, Prendergast exploited the white paper deliberately to intensify the sunlit brilliance of a scene, as in the case of the* Café Florian *(No. 82).*

76 ITALIAN FLOWER MARKET   1898
Pencil and water color, 14½ x 10 inches
Signed lower right in pencil: *Prendergast*
(formerly collections Mrs. Montgomery Sears, Mrs. J. D. Cameron Bradley)
Lent by Dr. and Mrs. Irving Levitt

77 UMBRELLAS IN THE RAIN, VENICE (Ponte della Paglia)   1899
(verso: unfinished study of same composition)
Pencil and water color, 13¾ x 20½ inches
Signed lower left in ink: *Prendergast / Maurice B. Prendergast Venice / 1899*
Lent by the Museum of Fine Arts, Boston

78 MARKET PLACE, VENICE ("Rialto")   1898
Pencil and water color, 13¾ x 10 inches
Signed lower right in ink: *Maurice B. Prendergast*
Lent by Mrs. Charles Prendergast

The figure in the foreground stands on the steps of the Rialto bridge with the Church of San Giacomo di Rialto at right.

79 FESTIVAL DAY, VENICE   1899
Pencil and water color, 13 x 21 inches
Signed lower left in pencil: *Prendergast*
Lent by Mt. Holyoke College, Dwight Art Memorial

80 SUNLIGHT ON THE PIAZZETTA, VENICE   1899
Pencil and water color, 12½ x 20⅝ inches
Inscribed lower left in pencil: *Prendergast / Venice*
Lent by Mr. and Mrs. William T. Aldrich

(87)

80 SUNLIGHT ON THE PIAZZETTA, VENICE   1899

81 PROCESSION, VENICE   1898–99
Pencil and water color, 11 x 12¼ inches
Signed lower right in ink: *Prendergast*
(formerly collection Mrs. C. Nichols Greene)
Lent by Mr. and Mrs. John G. Greene

82 CAFÉ FLORIAN, VENICE   1899
Water color, 10¼ x 14¾ inches
Signed lower left in ink: *Maurice Prendergast*
Lent by Mrs. Charles Prendergast

83 RHODODENDRONS, BOSTON PUBLIC GARDEN   1899
Pencil and water color, 13⅞ x 20½ inches
Signed lower left in ink: *Maurice B. Prendergast . . / 1899 . .*
Lent by Mrs. Charles Prendergast

84 CARNIVAL (Franklin Park, Boston)   about 1900
Pencil and water color, 13 x 14½ inches
Unsigned
Lent by the Museum of Fine Arts, Boston
    (Gift of the Estate of Nellie P. Carter)

85 MERRY-GO-ROUND (Nahant)   1900
("Carousel")
Pencil and water color, 13¾ x 19⅞ inches
Signed lower left: *Prendergast*
Lent by the Museum of Fine Arts, Springfield, Mass.

86 THE STONY BEACH (Ogunquit)   1901
Pencil and water color, 20¾ x 13½ inches
Signed lower left: *Prendergast*
Lent by Dr. and Mrs. MacKinley Helm

(89)

The title derives from the original label of the Pan American Exposition, Buffalo, whereon the artist is listed as owner with the address of 83 Walnut Street, Winchester. A Walter Kimball and Company label also on the painting gives the title as "Scene at Ogunquit." Two small oils with the title "Brooksville, Maine" (in the Penobscot Bay area near Blue Hill) testify to the fact that Prendergast painted in Maine at a later date, probably after the 1909–10 Paris trip. There is additional evidence of a later visit in the pastel Beach Late Afternoon, Maine (No. 116). Prendergast was certainly in Maine at an earlier date as evidenced by three water colors of 1889 painted at Brook's Cove, Westport Lower Landing.

87 CENTRAL PARK (New York)   1901
    Pencil and water color, $14^{1}/_{8} \times 21^{3}/_{4}$ inches
    Inscribed lower left in ink: *Maurice B. Prendergast / Central Park 1901*
    Lent by the Whitney Museum of American Art

    The composition is related to Bonnard's lithograph "Boulevard" (R.M 61). A variant, also in the Whitney Museum, is the water color inscribed The Bridle Path, Central Park, *1902, portraying Olmstead's ingenious three-way transportation system with carriage road, bridle path and pedestrian walk in three parallel tiers. This was further developed in the oil painting in the Metropolitan Museum,* Central Park *in 1903.*

88 MAY DAY, CENTRAL PARK (New York)   1901
    Pencil and water color, $13^{7}/_{8} \times 19^{3}/_{4}$ inches
    Inscribed at bottom in ink: *Maurice B. Prendergast*
        Central Park 1901 / New York
    Lent by the Cleveland Museum of Art (J. H. Wade Collection)

89 MAY DAY, CENTRAL PARK (New York)   about 1901
    Pencil and water color, $14^{3}/_{8} \times 21^{5}/_{8}$ inches
    Signed lower right: *Prendergast*
(90)   Lent by the Whitney Museum of American Art

84 CARNIVAL about 1900   (91)

A close variant of this water color, in a slightly paler tonality, is in a private collection in Boston. Two other notable water colors of the Central Park theme are the Addison Gallery's In Central Park *with the circular fountain and the* Sailboat Pond, Central Park *in the collection of Mrs. John F. Kraushaar.*

90   THE MALL (Central Park, New York)   1901
Pencil and water color, 22 x 20 inches
Signed lower right in ink: *Maurice B. Prendergast*
Lent by Margarett Sargent McKean

91   THE MALL, CENTRAL PARK (New York)   1901
Pencil and water color, $14^1/_8$ x $21^1/_4$ inches
Inscribed lower right in pencil: *Maurice B. Prendergast / The Terrace Bridge*
    Central Park / 1901 New York
Lent by the Art Institute of Chicago
    (Gift of Annie Swan Coburn in memory of Olivia Shaler Swan)

92   THE EAST RIVER (New York)   1901
Pencil and water color, $13^3/_4$ x $19^3/_4$ inches
Inscribed lower right in ink:
    Maurice B. Prendergast / 1901 The East River
Lent by the Museum of Modern Art (Gift of Mrs. John D. Rockefeller, Jr.)

93   MADISON SQUARE, NEW YORK   1901
Pencil, pen und water color, 15 x $16^3/_8$ inches
Signed lower right in ink:
    Madison Square / New York / Maurice B. Prendergast / 1901
Lent by Mrs. Charles Prendergast

94   MULBERRY BEND PARK (New York)   about 1901
Pencil and water color, unfinished, $14^1/_2$ x $21^1/_2$ inches
Inscribed lower right in pencil: *Prendergast / Mulbery Bend*
Lent by Mr. and Mrs. Richard K. Weil

85 MERRY-GO-ROUND 1900   (93)

95 COLUMBUS CIRCLE (New York)   about 1903
Water color, 14 x 23 inches
Signed lower right: *Prendergast*
Lent by Mr. and Mrs. Harry Rubin

96 PROMENADE (ON THE PIER), NANTASKET   1905
Pencil and water color, 12¼ x 19 inches
Signed lower right in ink: *Prendergast*
Lent by the Addison Gallery of American Art, Phillips Academy, Andover

97 APRIL SNOW, SALEM   1906–07
Pencil and water color, 14³/₄ x 21⁵/₈ inches
Signed lower left: *Prendergast*
Lent by the Museum of Modern Art (Gift of Mrs. John D. Rockefeller, Jr.)

98 DOCKS, EAST BOSTON   1908–09
("Docks, South Street, New York")
Pencil and water color, 14½ x 21¼ inches
Signed lower left in pencil: *Prendergast*
(formerly collection Arthur F. Egner)
Lent by Winthrop F. Taylor

*This water color was listed in the Whitney Museum Memorial
Exhibition, 1934, No. 19 (ill.), under the above title; the Addison Gallery
exhibition catalogue, 1938, No. 32, gives the title as Docks, South Street,
New York. Identification is perhaps more contingent on the competitive claims
of the two cities for shipping enterprise than on recognizable landmarks.*

99 WEST CHURCH, BOSTON   1909
Pencil and water color, 21¾ x 15 inches
Unsigned
Lent by the Society for the Preservation of New England Antiquities

The West Church, also called the Bartol Church after its dynamic minister,
may still be seen at the corner of Cambridge and Lynde Streets, and has been

recently a branch of the Boston Public Library. It was built by Asher Benjamin in 1806. Van Wyck Brooks relates that Mrs. Bartol had commissioned Prendergast to do a water color of the church, and the artist, intrigued by the faded green-blue doors, saved them for the last, only to have two house painters step in and repaint the doors a cold raw blue.

100 WEST CHURCH, BOSTON about 1909
Pencil, water color, and opaque white, 10½ x 15¼ inches
Signed lower right in wash: *Prendergast*
Lent by the Museum of Fine Arts, Boston

A larger variant, more freely painted, is in the Metropolitan Museum, while a view of the fountain courtyard seen in reverse from the steps of the church looking across Cambridge Street appeared in the Parke-Bernet Galleries sale catalogue of the collection of Mrs. Cornelius J. Sullivan, December 1939, No. 35.

101 NOTRE DAME, PARIS 1909
Pencil and water color, 13^{13}/$_{16}$ x 10^{15}/$_{16}$ inches
Signed lower right: *Maurice Prendergast*
Lent by the Worcester Art Museum

102 MONTPARNASSE (Paris) about 1909
Water color and body color, 13^{3}/$_{8}$ x 19^{5}/$_{8}$ inches
Signed lower right in pencil: *Prendergast*
(formerly collection Arthur Bradley Campbell)
Lent by Mr. and Mrs. M. P. Potamkin

103 BOAT LANDING, DINARD 1909
Water color mixed with opaque white, with outlines in charcoal
13^{3}/$_{8}$ x 20^{3}/$_{8}$ inches
Signed lower right with brush in red-brown: *Prendergast*
(Inscribed on verso in charcoal: St. Malo, 1909)
Lent anonymously

97 APRIL SNOW, SALEM 1906-07

104 THE BALLOON (Paris) 1910
Pencil and water color, 13½ x 19½ inches
Signed lower right in pencil: *Maurice Prendergast*
Lent by the Addison Gallery of American Art, Phillips Academy, Andover

105 BEACH, ST. MALO 1910
Pencil and water color, 16³/₈ x 13³/₈ inches
Signed lower right with brush: *Prendergast*
Lent by Mrs. John F. Kraushaar

106 PROMENADE (France) 1909–10
Pencil and water color, 12¾ x 10½ inches
Signed lower left in ink: *Prendergast*
Lent anonymously

107 SANTA MARIA FORMOSA, VENICE 1912
Pencil and water color, 21½ x 14¾ inches
Inscribed lower left in ink: *Maurice B. Prendergast / Venice / 1912*
Lent by the Museum of Fine Arts, Boston

108 TWO GIRLS IN NEW ENGLAND WOODLAND about 1912
Pencil and water color, 12 x 18 inches
Signed lower right of center in ink: *Prendergast*
Lent by Mrs. Sherman Miles

109 CAPE ANN about 1912–14
Pencil and water color, 9½ x 13 inches
Signed lower right in ink: *Prendergast*
Lent by the Museum of Fine Arts, Boston

110 ALONG THE COAST about 1912–14
water color, 15³/₈ x 22 inches
Signed lower right in ink: *Prendergast*
Lent by Mr. and Mrs. Henry Lee, Jr.

(97)

This and a water color in the Cleveland Museum, The Rocky Seashore, *are significant for their elemental intensity of expression, unrelieved by human presence, perhaps inspired by the more structural brush strokes of Cézanne.*

111 THE RIDER about 1914
Pencil and water color, 9³/₈ x 11¹/₂ inches
Signed lower right in ink: *Prendergast*
(formerly collection John Quinn)
Lent by Mr. and Mrs. John G. Pierce

The water color in the Brooklyn Museum, Composition with Figures *(formerly collection John Quinn), was inspired from sketches of Egyptian tomb paintings in imitation of mosaic. Prendergast executed several small panels in colored mosaic.*

112 BEACH SCENE WITH FIGURES about 1914
Pencil and water color, 13³/₄ x 19¹/₂ inches
Signed lower right in ink: *Prendergast*
(formerly collections Charles Prendergast, Charles Downing Lay)
Lent by Mr. and Mrs. George Greenspan

113 DECORATIVE COMPOSITION 1914
(Study for *Promenade,* No. 34, in Detroit Institute)
Pencil and water color, 12 x 20¹/₄ inches
Signed lower left in ink: *Prendergast*
(formerly collection John Quinn)
Lent by Joseph H. Hirshhorn

114 THE BATHERS about 1914-16
Pencil and water color, 10¹/₂ x 14³/₄ inches
Signed lower left in ink: *Prendergast*
(formerly collection John Quinn)
Lent by Mr. and Mrs. John G. Pierce

100 WEST CHURCH, BOSTON about 1909   (99)

115   EIGHT GIRLS BY THE SEA   1914-18
Pencil and water color, 8 x 15 inches
Signed lower right in ink: *Prendergast*
(formerly Lewisohn Collection)
Lent by Dr. and Mrs. Ernest Kahn

116   BEACH LATE AFTERNOON, MAINE   about 1916
Pastel, 14¾ x 21¾ inches
Signed lower right in pencil: *Maurice B. Prendergast*
(formerly collection Joseph Katz)
Lent by the Museum of Fine Arts, Boston

117   BEACH WITH BLUE TREE   1917–18
Charcoal and water color mixed with opaque white, $13^{3}/_{8}$ x $19^{3}/_{8}$ inches
Signed lower right with brush in gray wash: *Prendergast*
Lent by Mrs. Charles Prendergast

118   HORSE AND WAGON   about 1917–20
Pencil and water color, 11¼ x 13¾ inches
Signed lower left with brush in red wash: *Prendergast*
Lent anonymously

119   PICNIC GROVE   about 1918
Pencil and water color, 14½ x 20 inches
Signed lower right in ink: *Maurice B. Prendergast*
Lent by Mr. and Mrs. Arthur G. Altschul

120   IN THE PARK   1918–19
("Day in the Country")
Pencil and water color
Signed lower right in pencil: *Prendergast*
Lent by the Art Institute of Chicago
   (Gift of Annie Swan Coburn in memory of Olivia Shaler Swan)

(100)   *This was probably painted at Salem Willows.*

104 THE BALLOON 1910 (101)

121   THE RIDER   1919–20
Pencil and water color, $9^5/_8$ x $13^5/_8$ inches
Signed lower center in ink: *Prendergast*
Lent by the Metropolitan Museum of Art
   (Bequest of Margaret S. Lewisohn, 1954)

122   FOUR GIRLS IN MEADOW   about 1919–20
Pencil, water color and pastel, $14^3/_4$ x 18 inches
Signed lower right with brush: *Prendergast*
Lent by Mrs. Charles Prendergast

123   GOLF COURSE, EAST GLOUCESTER   1920
Pencil, water color and charcoal, $13^1/_2$ x $18^1/_2$ inches
Signed lower right with brush: *Prendergast*
Lent by the Addison Gallery of American Art, Phillips Academy, Andover

Monotypes

124   BASTILLE DAY (LE QUATORZE JUILLET)   1892
Color monotype on laid paper, $6^7/_8$ x $5^1/_8$ inches (comp.)
Scratched in plate at bottom: *Le Quatorze Juillet 1892:* $^P_{MB}$
Lent by the Cleveland Museum of Art (Gift of the Print Club of Cleveland)

*Assuming the inscribed date of 1892 to be the date of execution, as was
habitually Prendergast's practice, this may lay claim to being the earliest
dated monotype. It suggests an early relationship to Bonnard as is later
evidenced in the monotype* Tremont Street, Boston *(No. 137) and a study in
Prendergast's* Watercolor Sketchbook, 1899 *(No. 148) in the Boston Museum.
Both relate to Bonnards' suite of lithographs published in 1895,*
Quelques aspects de la Vie de Paris.

109   CAPE ANN   about 1912–14   (103)

125   SKIPPING ROPE   about 1895
Color monotype touched with pencil on cream japan paper, 5 x 10 inches (comp.)
Scratched in plate lower left: M.B.P.
Lent by Miss Daphne Dunbar

126   THE PRETTY SHIPS   about 1897
Color monotype on buff japan paper, $7 \times 6^3/_8$ inches (comp.)
Scratched in plate at bottom: *The Pretty Ships* $_{MB}^{P}$
(formerly collection Herman Dudley Murphy)
Lent by the Museum of Fine Arts, Boston

*The same title and composition occurs in a small oil on panel, 13½x14¼ inches,
which was in the New York art market in 1958.*

127   LADY IN PURPLE   about 1897
Color monotype on cream japan paper, 15 x 11 inches (sheet)
Monogram in pencil lower left: $_{B}^{MP}$
Lent by Robert Brady

128   SIX SKETCHES OF LADIES
Color monotype on buff japan paper, $14 \times 10^3/_4$ inches (sight),
pencil sketch in margin
Monogram scratched three times: $M \, _{B}^{P}$
Lent by Mr. and Mrs. Nelson Goodman

129   LADY IN PINK SKIRT
Color monotype on cream wove paper, $11 \times 7^1/_8$ inches (comp.)
Monogram in orange crayon lower left: $_{B}^{M} _{P}$
Lent by Mrs. Charles Prendergast

130   THE SPANISH STEPS (Rome)   about 1898
Color monotype on cream japan paper, $11^{11}/_{16} \times 7^1/_2$ inches (comp.)
Scratched in plate at bottom: *The Spanish Steps:* M:B:P

Lent by Miss Leona E. Prasse

131 THE ROMAN CAMPAGNA about 1899
Color monotype on cream wove paper, $9^1/_8 \times 12^3/_8$ inches (comp.)
Scratched in plate at bottom: *The Roman Campagna* $^{MB}_P$
Lent by the Des Moines Art Center (Truby Kelly Kirsch Memorial Collection)

132 ON THE CORSO, ROME about 1899
Color monotype on cream wove paper, $11^3/_4 \times 7^1/_2$ inches (comp.)
Scratched in plate at bottom: *Via delle:Corso:Rome* M.B.P.
Lent by Mr. and Mrs. Melvin Schifter

133 ORANGE MARKET about 1899
Color monotype, $12^1/_2 \times 9$ inches (comp.)
Monogram lower left: $^{MP}_B$
Lent by the Museum of Modern Art (Gift of Mrs. John D. Rockefeller, Jr.)

*Both subject and technique of this bold composition relate to Pissarro
who was an enthusiastic practitioner of the color monotype.*

134 DRESS REHEARSAL about 1900
Color monotype on cream japan paper, $12^1/_2 \times 9^1/_8$ inches (comp.)
Scratched in plate at bottom: *Dress Rehearsal . . . M. B. Prendergast*
Lent by Ethel Reiner

*A variant, printed also in rose, browns and greens and touched slightly
in pencil, is in the Museum of Modern Art.*

135 THE OLD SHIPYARD 1901
Color monotype on cream japan paper, $11^1/_4 \times 13^3/_4$ inches (comp.)
Scratched in plate at bottom: *1901   The Old Shipyard   Prendergast*
Lent by Mr. and Mrs. Ansley W. Sawyer, Jr.

*There is a preparatory pencil drawing in the Large Boston Public Garden
Sketchbook, about 1895–97, belonging to Mrs. Charles Prendergast*

136 SUMMER DAY 1901
Color monotype on white laid paper, $11^1/_8 \times 14$ inches (comp.)

(105)

Signed in red crayon lower right: *MBP 1901*
Lent by Mr. and Mrs. Nelson Goodman

137 TREMONT STREET, BOSTON about 1902
Color monotype on cream paper, 10½ x 13½ inches (comp.)
Signed in yellow brush lower left: *Prendergast*
Lent by the Addison Gallery of American Art, Phillips Academy, Andover

138 STREET SCENE, BOSTON 1902
Color monotype touched with pencil, 9 x 12¼ inches (comp.)
Unsigned
Lent by Mrs. Stanley B. Resor

139 NOUVEAU CIRQUE (Paris) 1902
Color monotype on white laid paper, 13⅞ x 13¾ inches (comp.)
Scratched in plate at bottom: *Nouveau Cirque   Prendergast*
Lent by Mrs. Charles Prendergast

A smaller upright version in the collection of Mrs. Charles Prendergast and an oblong version in the Museum of Fine Arts, Boston, both called Bareback Rider, *are variations of this theme. Another treatment of the circus ring is in the Baltimore Museum of Art.*

140 BAREBACK RIDER (Paris)
Color monotype on cream japan paper, 7⅝ x 5¾ inches (comp.)
Scratched in plate lower right: *M.B.P.*
Lent by the Cleveland Museum of Art (Dudley P. Allen Collection)

A preparatory pencil study of a horse and rider drawn in reverse is in the Large Boston Public Garden Sketchbook, about 1895–97, in the collection of Mrs. Charles Prendergast.

141 FISHING PARTY
Color monotype on japan paper, 8½ x 6½ inches (comp.)
Scratched in plate lower left: *M.B.P.*
Lent by Margarett Sargent McKean

142   PICNIC WITH RED UMBRELLA
      Color monotype on cream paper, 9¼ x 7½ inches (comp.)
      Signed in red crayon lower left: M B P
      Lent by Mrs. Alfred Curtis

143   GIRLS ON ESPLANADE
      Color monotype on heavy wove paper, 8 x 6¾ inches (comp.)
      Scratched in plate lower left: M.B.P.
      Lent by the Museum of Fine Arts, Boston

144   CHILDREN PLAYING ON THE BEACH   1905
      Color monotype on cream japan paper, 10⅝ x 10⅛ inches (comp.)
      Scratched in plate lower left: M.B.P.
      Lent by the Addison Gallery of American Art, Phillips Academy, Andover

Drawings and Sketchbooks

145   STUDY OF THREE GIRLS WITH SCARVES   about 1914
      Pencil on cream charcoal paper, 12¼ x 19 inches (sheet)
      Unsigned
      Lent by Mrs. Charles Prendergast

146   NUDE MODEL WITH DRAPERY   about 1914
      Pencil and water color on gray charcoal paper, 12⅜ x 9½ inches (sheet)
      Unsigned
      Lent by Mrs. Charles Prendergast

147   STUDY OF STANDING NUDE GIRL   about 1914
      Pencil on cream charcoal paper, 12¼ x 9½ inches (sheet)
      Unsigned
      Lent by Mrs. Charles Prendergast

148 SKETCHBOOK (Summer, Boston and North Shore, Mass.)   1899
7 x 7½ inches
Black linen cover with red and black stripes painted on gray canvas spine
48 leaves: 52 water colors; 36 pencil drawings; 1 color crayon drawing
Inscribed by Charles Prendergast inside front cover in red: *Sketches by Maurice Prendergast / 1899*
Lent by the Museum of Fine Arts, Boston (Gift of Mrs. Charles Prendergast)

A full-color facsimile edition of this Sketchbook has been published by the Boston Museum and the Harvard University Press.

149 SKETCHBOOK   1912–14
$8^3/_8$ x $6^3/_4$ inches
Black marble paper cover with Boston label
66 leaves: 18 pen drawings; 67 pencil drawings
Figure studies, nude models and outline sketches for paintings
Lent by Mrs. Charles Prendergast

150 SKETCHBOOK (North Shore, Mass.)   about 1914–18
$7^3/_4$ x 5 inches
Green marble paper cover with Boston label
92 leaves: 60 pencil drawings; 7 double-page water colors
Studies of Salem Willows, Gloucester, Annisquam, Rockport, etc.
Inscribed on first page: "The Dells"
Lent by the Cleveland Museum of Art (Gift of Mrs. Charles Prendergast)

151 SKETCHBOOK (Summer, New England Shore)   1914 and after
$7^3/_4$ x $5^1/_8$ inches
Brown marble paper cover with label
51 leaves: 59 pencil drawings; 7 double-page water colors; 1 double-page crayon drawing
Lent by Mrs. Charles Prendergast

1 (109)

(110)

2

11 (113)

26

(117)

(119)

33   (121)

(123)

61   (125)

(127)

(128) 76

Prendergast

(129)

(130)

(131)

3

15

7

4   (135)

24

27

25

32

39

36

40

49

52

50

53

55

54

56 (141)

67

69

Le Quatorze Juillet 1892

129

127

125

126 (151)

138

142

(154) 139

140

143

145

144

146 (155)

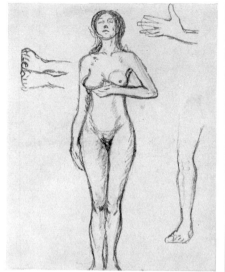

Sketchbooks Nos. 148 and 150 not illustrated.
No. 148, Water-Color Sketchbook, 1899, is
published in facsimile by the Museum of Fine Arts,
Boston and Harvard University Press, Cambridge,
1960, in conjunction with this exibition.

149